How to Sell Your
Home in Any Market—With or
Without a Broker

Also by Peter G. Miller

Successful Real Estate Negotiation
(with Douglas M. Bregman, Esq.)
Successful Real Estate Investing
Buy Your First Home Now
The Common-Sense Mortgage
(How to Cut the Cost of Home Ownership by $100,000 or More)

How to Sell Your Home in Any Market—With or Without a Broker

Peter G. Miller

HarperCollins*Publishers*

Library of Congress Cataloging-in-Publication Data
Miller, Peter G.
    How to sell your home in any market : with or without a broker / Peter G. Miller. — 1st ed.
        p.   cm.
    Includes index.

    1. House selling. I. Title.
    HD1379.M598   1994
333.33'83—dc20   93-33066

To Amanda, Sam, and Caroline

Contents

Acknowledgments

This book is the product of more than fifteen years of interest and experience in the real estate field as a journalist, broker, speaker, and author.

In Chapter 1, figures relating to mortgage tax deductions were obtained by using statistics on pages 1,045 and 1,046 of the *1992 Green Book*, a publication of the Committee on Ways and Means of the U.S. House of Representatives.

The 1983 Federal Trade Commission information cited in Chapter 1 was obtained from page 22 of a staff report by the FTC's Los Angeles regional office entitled, "The Residential Real Estate Brokerage Industry."

Information concerning home-value appreciation between 1970 and 1990 found in Chapter 1 is based on a story and chart published in *USA Today* (June 7, 1990) discussing a Salomon Bros., Inc., report on investment results.

Statistics in Chapter 1 showing that earnings for upper-income households rose eight times faster than average households can be found in the article "Who Paid the Most Taxes in the 80's? The Superrich," *The New York Times*, May 31, 1992.

Portions of the material concerning new tax write-off proposals in Chapter 1 was originally written for July/August, 1992, issue of *The Real Estate Professional* (Suite 5, 1492 Highland Avenue, Needham, MA 02192).

Information in Chapter 4 relating to alternative real estate commissions was first developed in materials published privately by the author in 1981.

The material on nonhomogeneity in Chapter 5 was first mentioned in a speech given by the author at the 20th annual Canadian-American Seminar in Windsor, Ontario, November 9–10, 1978, and subsequently published in the seminar proceedings, and in materials privately published by the author.

Randy Hertz of Hertz Farm Management (Nevada, Iowa) provided information in Chapter 5 concerning farm sales.

The concept of hidden marketing issues discussed in Chapter 5 originated in seminars given by the author, and in a weekly column written by the author and published in *The Washington Post* (June 25, 1977).

The owner's fix-up rule discussed in Chapter 6 is widely used within the real estate industry. The author heard about the fix-up rule concept in the 1970s and has used it in seminars and articles since then.

Information regarding owner home-sale preferences (Chapter 7), down-payment statistics (Chapter 11), the division of homesellers between Fizzbos and those who use a broker (Chapter 2), and the box on Fizzbo choices (Chapter 3) are taken from *The Homebuying and Selling Process, 1991*, a study published by the National Association of Realtors and used in this guide with permission.

Material in Chapter 11 on open-house preparations was drawn in part from a weekly column dated November 5, 1977, and published by the author in *The Washington Post*.

In Chapter 11, material on words not to use in real estate marketing were derived from materials produced by the Human Relations Commission of Montgomery County, Maryland, and from materials written by the author and posted within the real estate area of America Online, a nationwide electronic bulletin board.

The material in Chapter 11 regarding preparing open houses; working with explorers, brokers, and buyers; and other matters were developed in seminars given by the author and in columns written by the author for *The Washington Post*.

The concept of the negotiation zones and certain ideas relating to the use of addenda in Chapter 13 as well as material in Chapter 14 concerning musts, shoulds, and extras were originally used in *Successful Real Estate Negotiation* (HarperPerennial), a guide co-authored with Douglas M. Bregman, Esq., an attorney based in Bethesda, Maryland, with the firm of Bregman, Berbert & Schwartz. As well, the material on addenda (Chapter 13) follows ideas and concepts developed in the negotiation book.

I particularly thank my negotiation co-author, Douglas M. Bregman, for permitting reproduction of glossary material from *Successful Real Estate Negotiation* in this guide.

The material on taxation and tax concepts was reviewed by Mr. Jeffrey A. Stoltz, a certified public accountant based in Bethesda, Maryland, with the firm of Osterman & Stoltz, Chartered.

I want to thank Jeff Lubar, vice president, public affairs, and Elizabeth Duncan, director of media relations, National Association of Realtors, for their willingness to answer questions and provide research materials. Readers should be aware that the term "Realtor" is a registered collective membership mark that may be used only by members of the National Association of Realtors.

I am grateful to Deborah S. Kreiser for her careful reading of the original manuscript, and I want to thank Robert A. Kaplan, senior editor at HarperCollins, for his suggestions, support, and confidence.

Lastly, I thank my agent, Marcy Posner of the William Morris Agency in New York, for her efforts on my behalf.

Preface

This book all began in the 1970s when I wanted to sell my first home.

It took about three weeks as a self-seller and the price I received resulted in the largest check—payable to me—that I had ever seen. Thus my interest in real estate was ignited.

Over the years I have seen things change. Real estate marketing has become decidedly more complex, brokers and agents are better trained, far more consumer information is available, legal advice is increasingly necessary, and the marketplace itself has become progressively adversarial.

Not only are real estate deals more difficult to complete on a technical basis, they are also more difficult because the marketplace has evolved. Homes in many communities are no longer salable on a moment's notice. Values do not always soar. Some values—like stock and bond prices—fall.

This book explores real estate marketing and the logical, effective, tested steps homeowners can take to get the best possible price and terms for his or her property. It is not a book that particularly favors one form of marketing or another; instead the idea is to examine available options, explain the pros and cons in plain English, and let you make the decisions that best fit your needs and preferences.

Ultimately it is your best interests that are on the line, reason enough to plan the sale of your home with care and caution. This book is designed to help in your marketing process because it follows the experiences and sequence most homesellers encounter.

The book is written in a modular fashion so that you can pick and choose the areas most interesting to you. The modular concept also makes the book ideal for real estate and consumer classes because instructors can review those sections of the text most appropriate to classroom work.

This guide is designed as a companion to other books in this series: *The Common-Sense Mortgage, Buy Your First Home Now, Successful Real Estate Negotiation* (with Douglas M. Bregman, Esq.), and *Successful Real Estate Investing*, all by HarperPerennial.

You are about to embark on an interesting journey, one filled with choices, chances, and financial opportunity. I wish you every possible success, and I hope as well that this guide helps you gain a new title: home-seller.

Peter G. Miller

How to Sell Your Home in Any Market—With or Without a Broker

This publication is intended solely as a general overview of selected issues commonly associated with the sale, purchase, and financing of residential real estate. The author and the publisher make no representations with respect to the contents hereof and specifically disclaim any implied or express warranties of merchantability or fitness for any particular usage, application, or purpose.

"This publication is designed to provide accurate and authoritative information in regard to the subject matter covered. It is sold with the understanding that the publisher is not engaged in rendering legal, accounting, or other professional services. If legal advice or other expert assistance is required, the services of a competent professional person should be sought." *(From a Declaration of Principles jointly adopted by a Committee of the American Bar Association and a Committee of Publishers.)*

Figures used throughout the text, in various charts, and in amortization statements are for illustrative purposes only and have been rounded in most cases. Readers should consult with appropriate sources for precise figures when computing mortgage amortization statements and other information.

Names, characters, places, and incidents used in examples throughout this book are fictitious. Any resemblance to actual persons, living or dead, or to actual places or events is purely coincidental.

1
Selling in the New Era

For much of the past 50 years, selling the American home has been an adventure with few losers. Buy now, sell later, and pocket big money. The great wealth machine rarely failed, and if it did you could always catch up with the next deal.

But what used to be the American dream has turned sour for a growing army of homeowners. The little house with the white picket fence—and its related condos, co-ops, townhouses, track homes, mini-mansions, and farms—is no longer home sweet home. Economic studies, anecdotal reports, national surveys, and common observation all confirm the same view: the superheated markets of the 1980s are gone, dead, and buried. Selling a home is no longer the sure bet it once was.

Why has the real estate market changed? What can owners do to sell properties quickly and at premium prices?

These are crucial questions, and they are asked frequently. More than 3,000,000 existing homes are sold each year, and for many owners the selling process is now lengthy, discomforting, costly, and psychologically draining—the mortar-and-bricks equivalent of a root canal.

The troubles seen by sellers in recent years will continue because real estate sales and values reflect a variety of underlying national trends. Unfortunately, many of the unpleasant trends now in place seem destined to stay with us for years to come.

THE NEW ECONOMICS

The movement of jobs and technology overseas has already changed the relationship between labor and management—workers rarely strike, employees are less secure, and pay raises and perks are increasingly tough to earn. Workplace economics have created a vast and observable public discomfiture, precisely the financial environment least likely to inspire consumer confidence and the willingness to make major buying decisions. Homeownership—once the stuff of dreams—is increasingly seen as risky in an era when mortgage payments are certain but tomorrow's paycheck is not.

Massive debt owed by individuals, corporations, and every level of government chokes economic growth and constricts policy choices. Making matters worse, overseas money from Japan, Germany, and the Middle East is drying up, reducing the supply of capital available to borrowers.

Property values have increased faster than inflation during the past twenty years. Salomon Brothers, in its widely publicized analysis of various investment choices, states that during the period from 1970 through 1990, real estate values rose 7.4 percent annually compared with a 6.2 percent increase in the yearly cost of living.

At first an annual difference of 1.2 percent may not seem important. Over twenty years, however, the difference adds up. A home bought for $100,000 in 1970 would be worth $330,035 by 1990 if it appreciated at 6.2 percent annually. The same house, appreciating at 7.4 percent over the same period, would be valued at $416,952. The difference between the two values—$86,917—represents real wealth, buying power beyond the rate of inflation.

As good as real estate has been, the example above greatly understates how homeownership creates wealth. The home that cost $100,000 in 1970 was probably bought with a mortgage. If a purchaser put down 10 percent and financed the balance, then the monthly mortgage payments can be regarded as a form of economic rent (because the owner had to live somewhere), while the down payment can be seen as an investment.

Looking at the rate of return from this perspective, a $10,000 investment grew to $316,952 in twenty years. The annual rate of return aver-

How Real Estate Wealth Is Created		
	Cost of Living	Typical Home
Price, 1970	$100,000	$100,000
Annual Increase	6.2 percent	7.4 percent
Home Price, 1990	$330,035	$416,952
Difference	Not Appropriate	$86,917

aged 18.86 percent on an investment with minimal risk and substantial tax advantages.

The economics of real estate ownership have powered the marketplace for many years because homes have typically represented an appreciating asset. If hard times mean that real estate values increase at or about the rate of inflation—or less—then much of the investment rationale is lost and the urge to own plummets. If fewer buyers enter the marketplace, there is less competition for homes and little pressure pushing up prices. For homesellers, such conditions translate into reduced expectations, less profit, more concessions, and a marketing process that is likely to drag on for months.

TAXES

For many years Uncle Sam has used tax deductions as a lever to encourage people to buy homes and to buy often. There is little doubt that many people who might be perfectly content as renters today own homes precisely because real estate economics have been tilted by federal tax policies.

And there is little doubt as well that sellers have benefited enormously from federal tax policies. Tax benefits bring more people into the real estate marketplace. More buyers mean more demand and demand pushes up prices and creates a greater certainty that homes will sell.

But what if tax policies change? What if mortgage interest and property taxes are no longer deductible? Will there be as many buyers in the marketplace? Will home values hold up?

If you pay $10,000 a year in mortgage interest and write off 28 percent, it means your real interest cost is $7,200—a much more acceptable figure. Seen another way, if you pay 7.5 percent interest but deduct 28 percent of your home mortgage costs, then the effective interest rate after taxes is reduced to 5.4 percent.

The government's tax policies do not put more cash in your pocket. If you have a home mortgage and write off $5,000, that's money paid to lenders rather than to the federal government. What tax policies really do is give consumers the right to choose how they want their money spent. You can invest in property (in the case of mortgage write-offs), or you can give your money to Uncle Sam and let the government use it. Most people, for obvious reasons, are not thrilled at the thought of sending still more money to the government.

In 1992, for example, an estimated 25.8 million taxpayers wrote off mortgage-interest deductions worth $40.8 billion.

The catch is that not everyone deducts the same amount. One percent of the nation's taxpayers, those making $200,000 a year or more, subtracted mortgage-interest costs worth $4.77 billion from their tax bills in 1991, according to the Joint Committee on Taxation. In contrast, deductions valued at $2.76 billion were claimed by the 57.7 percent of all taxpayers who make less than $30,000 a year.

Juggle the numbers any way you want, there is no question that the rich are getting a huge share of all mortgage deductions.

The disproportionate nature of mortgage write-offs is hardly surprising, because the rich pay an outsized share of all home mortgage interest. Despite the unremarkable equation—big payments equal big deductions—there is a growing perception that mortgage write-offs for the well-to-do are inherently unfair.

The basic beef among those who oppose big mortgage write-offs is the glaring disparity among the homes of the rich and the residences of the poor and—for the sake of politics—the middle class. Somehow, it is argued, the government should not effectively subsidize the wealthy by allowing them to enjoy large mortgage deductions.

Combine big write-offs for the wealthy, the need for decent housing among the poor, tax relief for the middle class, revenue shortages at all levels of government, and you can guess what's next: an effort to cap or end interest write-offs for the upper crust, folks with incomes that rose eight times faster than average wage earners' between 1977 and 1989.

One idea is to limit mortgage write-offs to a politically tolerable figure, say $20,000 a year. At 7.5 percent interest, only those with mortgage debt of more than $266,666 would be touched. Most people—and most voters—would surely approve a system that raises someone else's taxes.

But if there is a cap on mortgage write-offs, you know what will follow: the cap that is $20,000 today will stay at $20,000 even as inflation creates seemingly steeper home prices that require bigger mortgages. As more and more people bump into a mortgage cap down the road, demand will drop and home sales will dip because real estate will hold less economic attraction.

People with adjustable-rate mortgage (ARM) financing who are not among the captains of high finance may also hit the $20,000 mark if interest rates soar. At 10.5 percent interest—a common rate in the 1980s—a mortgage balance in excess of $190,500 would be enough to break a $20,000 interest cap. And if rates go to 12 percent—something permitted by many current ARMs—then a middle-class borrower with as little as $166,700 in mortgage debt will suddenly have interest payments that are not deductible.

It is equally possible that the $20,000 limitation will change. The $20,000 cap that may seem so reasonable today (at least for the majority of people among the non-rich) could evolve into a different number in the future, say $19,000 one year, $18,000 the next, and so forth. If this seems unlikely, consider that income-tax rates first imposed in 1913 were calculated at 3 percent of the first $10,000 earned by a taxpayer and 5 percent of everything higher. In effect, once a taxing principle is established, there are always compelling reasons to change the numbers.

For homesellers, the problem with tax-code fiddling is unsettling: *Tax benefits make homeownership more affordable, so to the extent that write-offs are reduced, ownership—and homebuying—are that much less attractive.*

INFLATION

Since the end of World War II, American houses have grown bigger and bigger. The oddity of this trend is that family size has generally declined, so in effect homeowners have more living space than in the past.

More space is certainly a luxury, but one may suspect that luxury alone is not the reason behind the new crop of larger homes and mini-mansions. The real reason is money.

If real estate is an appreciating asset that can be bought with little money down, then it makes sense to buy the biggest house you can find—especially when you can also get big tax write-offs.

But if homes are not appreciating at or above the rate of inflation, then the equation changes. If the rate of inflation is 3 percent and an asset appreciates 2 percent per year, then buying power—real wealth—is being lost. This illustration becomes less clear when dealing with houses, however, because of leverage.

If Thompson buys a home for $100,000 and puts down 10 percent, his cash investment is $10,000. The money he pays for mortgage costs and the interest lost on his $10,000 down payment are actually a form of rent, because Thompson has to live somewhere.

One Deal, Four Views	
Thompson's Property	
Market-Value Approach	
Purchase Price:	$100,000
2 Percent Appreciation	$2,000
Market Value	$102,000
Investment Approach	
Down Payment	$10,000
Equity Growth	$2,000
Total Equity	$12,000
Equity Increase	20 percent
Inflation Approach	
Purchase Price	$100,000
Equity Increase	$2,000
Market Value	$102,000
Less: 3 Percent Inflation	$3,060
After-Inflation Value	$98,940
Buying-Power Approach	
Down Payment	$10,000
Equity Increase	$2,000
Total Before Inflation	$12,000
Less: 3 Percent Inflation	$360
Buying Power	$11,640
Rate of Return (1 Year)	16.4 percent

If the value of Thompson's property appreciates 2 percent, then it's "worth" $102,000 without considering sale expenses.

Since Thompson only put in $10,000, and since his equity is now $12,000 ($10,000 in a down payment plus $2,000 in appreciation), the value of his investment (the $10,000 paid up front) has actually increased 20 percent—at least on a cash basis.

If inflation is at 3 percent, then Thompson's property—in terms of buying power—has lost money. It's now worth $98,940 ($102,000 less 3 percent). Investment results are different, however, because Thompson's $10,000 investment has increased to $12,000. Less 3 percent inflation, Thompson's buying power has grown to $11,640—enough for an after-inflation return of 16.4 percent.

The catch is that while Thompson has increased his buying power, such newfound wealth is not immediately spendable. He has a greater net worth, but it hasn't made his checking account any larger. Also, selling real estate can involve expenses for marketing, taxes, and many other costs. The result is that small real estate "profits" are likely to be eaten up in the marketing process.

Thompson's property produced appreciation, but just like stocks and bonds, not every home will go up in value.

Suppose Green also buys a $100,000 home and also puts down $10,000. Unlike Thompson, Green doesn't do as well and the value of his property declines by 2 percent. At the same time, inflation is 3 percent, a factor that adds to Green's woes.

After one year, Green's situation looks like this: the market value of his home is $98,000 ($100,000 less 2 percent). The buying power represented by $98,000 is $95,060 ($98,000 less 3 percent inflation). As to Green's $10,000 investment, it now buys goods and services worth just $9,506 ($10,000 less 2 percent is $9,800; $9,800 devalued by 3 percent inflation means it is worth $9,506).

Leverage is a great and wonderful financial device, but it is a device that works when markets go up and also when they go down. Since leverage works both ways, in an environment without appreciation or with an actual drop in value, the bigger the house, the greater the loss. Green saw the value of a $100,000 home drop to $95,060, but if Green were among the rich and famous and owned a $1 million property, his loss would total almost $50,000.

Thus a down market is not equal for everyone. While there is almost always a market for entry-level houses, the appeal of larger properties is not so certain because the bigger the home, the bigger the potential loss.

In addition, at a time when family size is declining, few would-be owners want homes with 4,000 square feet and five or six bedrooms. Most families simply do not require such space, and if real estate values are stable or declining in the face of inflation, then owning a big property is a costly excess.

Some people, as a matter of personal preference, will opt for the largest home they can afford. But most people, most of the time, will look at their wallets when making a big purchase, an examination that will not help sellers if solid appreciation is missing from the home-buying equation.

NEW MARKET CONDITIONS

Not only are times tough and getting tougher, many of the marketplace advantages once enjoyed by sellers are gone.

It was not too long ago that homebuyers entered the marketplace at their peril. "Buyer beware" was an apt expression in an environment where virtually every custom, contract, and connection favored sellers.

A few years ago, for example, a typical sale worked like this: broker Smith listed a property and broker Jones brought in a buyer. Both Smith (the agent) and Jones (the subagent) worked for the seller and both were obligated to get the best possible price and terms for the owner.

Who worked for the buyer? In the usual case: no one. The buyer was a "customer" while the seller was the "client" or "principal" for whom a broker—and the broker's agents—were supposed to provide loyalty, performance, obedience, reasonable care, disclosure of material facts, and a proper accounting of papers and monies.

Buyers, as customers, were (and are) owed nothing but basic civility and fairness.

In practice the old system gave every possible advantage to the seller. To get current and past sale information, buyers usually worked with brokers and brokers usually were agents of a seller. Sales agreements contained clause after clause favoring the seller. Multiple listing services (MLSs) created relationships between brokers who listed properties and brokers who wanted to sell those listings. Many MLS systems literally banned participation by buyer representatives. Newspapers, supported by broker ads, rarely ran information that might alert buyers to their rights.

The system was so pervasive that a 1983 staff report from the Federal Trade Commission showed that 74 percent of all buyers thought realty brokers represented their interests. Ten percent somehow thought brokers represented both buyers and sellers at the same time!

The marketing system that once so strongly favored owners is now in disarray. More than 40 states presently require brokers to provide written disclosure statements stating up front and in clear language that they work for owners, unless there is a written agreement to the contrary. "Buyer brokerage," where brokers represent purchasers, is growing and the result is that more and more transactions are adversarial events where buyers and sellers each have their own champion.

As to the "buyer-beware" attitude that once dominated the marketplace, it's gone. Instead we have written disclosure forms, inspections, and—in too many cases—court suits and damages.

NEW ISSUES

While home sales were once relatively quick and easy, new issues have arisen that were unheard of 20 years ago. Radon tests, structural inspections, home-office zoning, wetlands restrictions, community regulations, and even the location of heliports have all evolved into contractual issues that can prolong a sale or lead to its demise.

The old days when buyers bought property with standardized (and one-sided) forms conveniently supplied by brokers are largely over, especially when more expensive properties are sold. Attorneys increasingly represent purchasers, which means buyers rely less and less on brokers for information and advice.

Complicating matters still further is the fact that even the relationship between sellers and brokers has evolved. Not too long ago, virtually all brokers used the same contract forms, belonged to the same MLS, used the same selling techniques, and charged the same fees. Bargaining over brokerage services was largely useless because every broker in town was likely to offer the same deal.

Today, brokers will negotiate both fees and arrangements—a consumer's dream unless one doesn't know what is negotiable or how to bargain. And since few brokerage agreements were negotiated in the past, public innocence in this area is unbounded.

OLD PERCEPTIONS, NEW REALITIES

Those who are now in the market as sellers were once active as buyers. The catch is that in the usual case, today's sellers were in the marketplace 10 or 12 years ago.

Owners thus offer their homes for sale in a radically changed environment. The experiences of the past are so outdated that they cannot possibly prepare a seller for today's marketplace realities. Financing, contracting, representation, warranties, marketing, licensure, disclosure, and economics have all evolved.

Sellers must unlearn the lessons of the past and absorb the new standards and conditions that dominate today's market. The process can be confusing, discomforting, and bewildering; it is also a process that can be profoundly expensive if not done correctly.

THE GOOD NEWS

There is little doubt that the real estate marketplace is less friendly to sellers now than at any time in recent memory. That said, there is no need to panic or become depressed. Owners still have many marketplace advantages that should not be overlooked.

While we are unlikely to see the go-go growth of the 1980s, our nation has a vast and wealthy internal market—the very type of market that countries in Europe and Asia are trying to duplicate. While unemployment may rise in tough times, most people in most places will be firmly employed.

The need for housing remains undiminished. Households are forming, immigrants arrive each day, and the population is growing. A broad trend toward caves and tents has not been spotted, and there is little doubt that the goal of homeownership remains firmly entrenched in the American psyche.

Financing, a central matter, has become increasingly accessible as programs for first-time buyers multiply, interest rates become increasingly tolerable, and such federal programs as Federal Housing Authority (FHA) mortgages and Veterans Administration (VA) loans remain widely available.

Most importantly, homes sell. Maybe they don't sell as quickly as in the past, maybe buyers are more aggressive than in prior years, but millions of homes are marketed annually.

The real question is not will your home sell, but what steps must you take to make it salable? What can you do to maximize the value of your property and how can you speed the selling process?

HOW TO USE THIS BOOK

This book is designed to help property owners sell homes whether markets are up or down and without regard to whether the sale is made directly by an owner or through a broker. It's not the purpose of this guide to suggest that one form of marketing is inherently superior to another, or to insist that there is but one path to selling success. All deals are different. Local markets are in constant flux. The skills and interests of individual sellers vary. The skills of individual brokers and agents differ.

Whether you wish to sell with a broker or independently, the choice is yours, but the odds of success in either case are vastly improved by understanding how the marketing process works and how you and your property fit into the system. It's the goal of this book to give you the information, background, and resources needed to make the decisions that work best for you.

2
How the System Works

Far out on the fringes of time, space, and commerce is a strange and complex netherworld where homes are bought and sold. Not a setting for the unwary, the real estate marketplace is a jumble of standards, trends, and illusions that can quickly plague the innocent and confound the unprepared.

But while the real estate marketplace is a morass of gimmicks and gambits, it is not unfathomable. Millions of homes are sold each year and the overwhelming probability is that your property can be successfully marketed. Less clear is how your property will be sold, by whom, and with what result.

Assuming you are sane, sober, old enough to vote, and otherwise legally competent, you have an absolute right to sell property as a "Fizzbo," someone selling "for sale by owner." In rough terms, 19 percent of all existing homes are sold by owners, while the rest are sold through the brokerage system according to the National Association of Realtors. Seen another way, four out of five sellers have brokers assist in the marketing process, assistance that raises a fundamental question: how do brokers get the right to represent your home in the marketplace?

LICENSURE

Homeselling is a regulated profession, which means that in the eyes of the law not everyone is qualified to market your home. The person you hire must have a license, and to get that license an individual must take certain classes and pass a standardized exam.

To see why a license is important, consider that cousin Lem can sell your house, but in the usual case he can't force you to pay a commission unless he has a real estate license. Thus the fundamental difference between having a license and not having a license is the ability to collect a fee in court, or—to put the matter more bluntly—to collect at all.

Licenses, according to those who regulate such matters, are created to "protect the public interest." The idea is to establish norms for education and experience so that when you hire a plumber, attorney, hairdresser, or whatever you can be certain that given standards have been met.

For the public, meaning for consumers, the licensing process should be seen as part of the national zeal for certification, something that is generally positive but is far from perfect. A license shows who passed a given set of standards, not who did best. Moreover, it is entirely possible that the established standards test the wrong issues or are not current. To deal with the latter problem, many regulated occupations now require continuing education courses as a condition of license renewal.

In the case of real estate brokerage there are two sets of licensure standards, one for brokers and one for salespeople, each with vastly different rights.

At the very top we have brokers, individuals "who for another and for a fee" are allowed to assist those who wish to purchase, sell, manage, exchange, or lease real property. While standards differ in each state, individuals generally cannot become brokers unless they have taken several college-level courses, passed a standardized test, and completed two to three years of experience. Of the roughly two million people with real estate licenses, a small minority—perhaps 10 to 15 percent—have broker status.

Buried in the description of a broker's license are important implications for homesellers.

- A broker can deal directly with the public and make contracts with individuals, corporations, and partnerships.
- A broker can work independently, with other brokers, or for other brokers.
- A broker can hire other brokers and salespeople.
- In some states, a real estate brokerage license enables individuals to sell both property and businesses.
- Brokers can set their own rates and fees.
- Brokers can establish their own business practices.
- In the event of a dispute, if a client fails to pay, brokers can sue to collect a fee or commission.

A broker's license is a valuable commodity, but most of the people you meet in real estate do not have such status. Instead, they are salespeople—folks known generally as "agents"—individuals with limited rights in the marketplace.

To become an agent one typically takes a basic course—say 30 to 100 classroom hours—and then a standardized test. In effect, you can get a sales license within two or three weeks in most states, a license that can allow you to earn substantial commissions.

If licensure sounds easy, it is. No college degrees are required, no lengthy apprenticeships, and no budget-busting tuition bills. While the real estate industry has been accused of many things, steep entry standards have never been an issue.

The fact that real estate is relatively easy to enter should be seen as good news for sellers. There are a huge number of people hustling for your business, and as Darwin told us, only the strong survive.

Agents, however, are not brokers. An agent cannot sell your home, collect a fee directly from a buyer or seller, or run a brokerage firm—at least not in his or her name. *An agent must work under the authority of a broker* and it is the broker who makes decisions, establishes policies, and sets fees.

To make the brokerage business even more interesting, agents typically act as "independent contractors." Unlike employees, independent contractors set their own hours, pay their own taxes, and underwrite their own benefits. It is thus possible to have a real estate firm with 100 agents where the broker employs no one, pays no unemployment taxes ("independent contractors" are not employees), and offers no benefits.

While entry standards are low, no broker with an interest in ongoing solvency will associate with agents who are not trained or competent. Brokers routinely offer classes and mentoring to assure that agents act prudently and ethically. If an agent makes an error, discriminates, or otherwise screws up, it is the broker who is responsible, the broker who can be liable for damages, and the broker who may lose his or her license and thus the ability to earn a living.

Once an individual has an agent's license, that person must take continuing education courses and pay renewal fees to maintain his or her standing. There is no requirement to move up to a broker's license, but after several years of experience, and with additional training, an agent can seek certification as a broker.

AGENCY

So far we have principals—such as homesellers or buyers—and we have brokers and their salespeople. Unmentioned as yet is how owners connect with brokers.

When you hire a broker, you retain someone to act on your behalf. There is a principal (you) and there is the person authorized to act in your place (the broker). This relationship is called "agency."

Agency can be created by the way people act, and it can also be created with written agreements. In the case of real estate, brokers want written agreements because then the nature and terms of their employment are clear. For the same reasons, you too want a written contract, what is known as a "listing agreement" in the real estate industry.

While the content and terms of a listing agreement are open to negotiation, the obligations created by an agency relationship are not. Plainly put, if someone is your agent they are obligated to act in your place and get the best possible price and terms available for your property.

An agent is not a neutral party, middleman, judge, go-between, intermediary, or mediator. Instead an agent is an advocate, someone required to place their principal's interests first and get the best possible deal for the party they serve.

Agency is a serious matter and individuals who act as agents must accept a series of important responsibilities.

- An agent must place the interests of the principal first.
- An agent must be loyal to his or her principal. The classic concept is that like a servant, an agent can only have one master.
- An agent must follow your instructions. As an example, you may decide that you don't want your home shown on Saturdays. A broker who accepts the listing is thus obligated to follow your instructions on this matter.
- An agent must use care to assure that your instructions are properly carried out.
- An agent must account for papers, contracts, and money held on your behalf.
- An agent must not exceed the authority you have granted. Unless otherwise agreed, hiring a broker to sell your home does not give him or her the right to sell your car or piano.

• An agent in most cases can only work for one party. For an agent to work for two principals at the same time means that he or she is a "dual agent." It is acceptable to be a *disclosed* dual agent, where both buyer and seller have agreed in advance to such an arrangement. But if a broker accidentally becomes a dual agent, then there are big problems.

How can one "accidentally" become a dual agent? Easy. Agency can be created by acts as well as written agreements. Thus, if buyer Powell thinks broker Conklin is his agent, relies on broker Conklin, gives confidential information to Conklin, views Conklin as "his" agent, and if broker Conklin does nothing to dissuade such views, then Conklin may well be regarded as Powell's agent.

But if Conklin is also an agent for seller Bertram, then there can be big problems because buyers and sellers have vastly different interests, goals, and motivations.

When there is an undisclosed dual agency, or a dual agency that is not approved in advance by both parties (and in writing to protect the broker), then the broker may be sued by the buyer, the seller, or both.

The problem of dual agency is particularly acute in a large brokerage firm that has many listings. If the property is listed by one salesman and sold by another, there is only one *broker* in the deal. With such in-house transactions brokers must use care to assure that buyers and sellers understand the broker's role or face the possibility of litigation.

Your agency relationship—if any—*must* be with a broker because only brokers may contract with the public. But the actual listing, showing, negotiating, and selling of your property may well be handled by a salesperson working under the broker's authority.

The agency relationship between sellers and brokers—and between brokers and salespeople—has important implications. Because a broker acts on your behalf, you can be liable for his or her actions (or inactions). And because salespeople are the broker's agents, the broker is responsible for them.

Thus agency creates a chain of relationships that leads to a potential chain of liability as well. If an agent working for your broker explains to buyers that the property is in a "restricted neighborhood and that Asians are not allowed to purchase homes in the community," good luck. The salesman (or saleswoman) is an agent of the broker and the broker may be responsible for such statements. The broker is your agent and so you can be held responsible for such comments and thus open to fines, damages, and other sanctions.

Because agency represents a potent string of liabilities, hiring an incompetent, inept, or biased broker can result in serious problems. Unless you have a strong desire to send the child of a needy lawyer through college, use care when choosing a broker.

LISTING AGREEMENTS

If you hire a broker to sell your home, that person typically acts as your agent. And an agent, as we have just seen, has important duties and obligations when serving a principal.

But what, exactly, is your relationship with a broker? How much are you going to pay this person and when is the money earned, due, and payable? Will your relationship with a broker continue until the property is sold, even if it doesn't sell for years?

To resolve these questions brokers will represent properties only with written listing agreements, employment contracts that outline the precise obligations of both brokers and owners. There are a variety of listing forms, and the type of agreement you accept should reflect how you want a sale handled.

Here, in general terms, are the basic forms of listing agreements used nationwide.

Open or General Listing. With this listing arrangement you give written permission for a broker to sell your home. There is no exclusivity, so one broker or 50 can hold open listings. If you sell the home by yourself, you will not owe a commission to brokers with an open listing.

Industry professionals dislike open listings because such agreements are less pro-broker than other listing formats. Open listings, however, do give authority to show a home, quote a given price, and collect a fee if all listing terms are met.

An open listing might be used in a situation when you're selling a home on your own, and broker Collins drops by an open house and says he has interested buyers.

You ask Collins about his buyers. What is their household income? How much down can they afford? Do they now have a house to sell or are they renting? (Don't ask the buyers' names—that's private information for the broker.)

If Collins refuses to answer or doesn't know, forget it. But if he can answer your questions, and if you want to list the property while you continue to sell, then an open listing may be appropriate.

Exclusive Agency Agreement. Brokers prefer an exclusive agency arrangement to an open listing because it greatly increases their chance to earn a fee. With an exclusive agency listing, you agree to list your home with one broker but you retain the right to sell by yourself.

With an exclusive agency agreement the listing broker will get a commission if he sells the property, and he will also get a commission if any other broker brings in a buyer. If you sell the property by yourself, however, the broker will not get a fee.

When considering an exclusive agency relationship, sellers should be aware that if they list with broker Phillips and sell through broker Giles, it is possible to owe *two* full commissions—one for each broker.

Why use an exclusive agency arrangement? Brokers—for obvious reasons—will not want to invest marketing dollars in a property with little potential to produce a commission. While an open listing can work well if a broker has a buyer in hand, an exclusive agency deal presumes that the broker will do some marketing and advertising.

Another reason to use an exclusive agency agreement concerns local multiple listing services (MLS). MLS systems will not accept open listings, but many will take exclusive agency deals. Thus, an exclusive agency arrangement can often get a property into an MLS, a valuable marketing asset.

Exclusive-Right-to-Sell Contract. This is the form of listing most eagerly sought by brokers, and with good reason—at least from their perspective. An exclusive-right-to-sell agreement says that if the property is sold during the listing period by the listing broker, another broker, you, or anyone, then the listing broker gets a fee.

The exclusive-right-to-sell agreement will get you into the local MLS if the listing broker belongs, and it should produce a sustained marketing effort from the broker—advertising, open houses (if appropriate), broker networking, mailings, signs, etc.

Multiple Listing Agreement. This is not a listing agreement per se, but rather an exclusive agency arrangement or an exclusive-right-to-sell contract that includes a provision requiring the broker to enter the property into one or more MLS systems.

HOW COMMISSIONS ARE EARNED

A listing shows that an owner and broker have a written agreement that defines their relationship. Part of that relationship is the obligation to pay the broker when his or her work is completed, an interesting subject in itself.

Most people, if asked, will say that a broker is hired to sell a house and that means a broker should be paid when a home is sold. *Brokers, however, are literally not hired to sell houses.* They are—according to the terms of most listing agreements—hired for another purpose: to find a buyer who is "ready, willing, and able" to purchase the property according to the precise and exact terms of the listing agreement.

Suppose Wilcox hires broker Gittens to sell his home for $345,000. If Gittens is successful, he will receive a commission equal to 5 percent of the sale price.

It takes some doing, but within a few weeks Gittens finds a buyer who wants the property, can afford the property, and is willing to make a written offer to pay the full $345,000. Wilcox hears about the buyer's interest and then turns around and tells Gittens, "Well, thank you very much, but I've decided I want $360,000 for the place."

We now have a mess. The employment contract between Wilcox and Gittens says that Gittens is to be paid when a buyer is found who is "ready, willing, and able" to purchase the property according to the precise and exact terms of the listing agreement. Gittens did what he was hired to do—he found a buyer who met the listing-agreement terms. The decision by Wilcox to raise the price is both interesting and irrelevant—a commission is earned, due, and payable because Gittens did his job.

The situation with Wilcox and Gittens is bizarre, but it does illustrate an important point: when a commission is owed, and when sellers think a commission is owed, can be confusing. In the usual case, several questions must be resolved to determine when a commission has been earned.

- Is the broker licensed?
- No license, no right to a commission.
- Is there a written listing agreement?

In theory, there can be an oral listing. But then, what are the terms of such an arrangement? Was the deal to sell the property for $200,000 or $210,000? Was the commission 3 percent or 9 percent? Was the oral listing canceled before the buyer was found? Who knows?

- Is the broker the efficient and procuring cause of sale?
- Did the broker "introduce" the buyer to the property and did that introduction set in motion a chain of events that led to the sale? For example, the Hendersons drive by a home on Fox Lane and see a "for sale" sign by the listing broker, Green Realty. The Hendersons contact broker Green, visit the property, and make an offer that is accepted by the seller. In this situation the sign "introduced" the Hendersons to the property and that introduction ultimately led to the sale.
- Is the buyer "ready, willing, and able" to purchase the property? No matter how much someone likes a property, such interest is irrelevant if it is not actionable. If buyer Noonan likes the Applegate house, that's great. But if the Applegate home costs $800,000 and Noonan has lousy credit and can't get a loan, then he is not "able" and won't be "ready" until he starts paying his bills.
- Have all listing terms been met?

This is a literal question; that is, if the listing says the property is for sale at $211,314 and an offer of $211,313 is received, the precise and exact terms of the listing have not been met, so no commission has been earned.

Most listing agreements, however, say that if the owner is willing to accept modified terms then the broker has earned a fee. This is a balanced and fair arrangement, especially since the owner cannot be compelled to accept anything other than the exact conditions stated in the listing.

Brokers are sometimes criticized because of the belief that somehow they magically and mysteriously earn vast amounts of money with little effort. A $250,000 home lists on Friday, sells on Sunday, and the broker pockets a $15,000 fee. The truth is that time and effort are not listing criteria. *Performance is the benchmark for brokers.* Either they perform or they don't, and if they do not fulfill every condition and requirement found in the employment agreement between themselves and sellers, then no payment is due regardless of the time, effort, or expense involved in a failed effort.

FEE SPLITTING

Now we know how fees are earned, but brokers commonly pocket far less than a complete commission. In many transactions, fees are split two ways, four ways, and sometimes even more.

Suppose you list your home for $200,000 with broker Kilbourne. You agree that if the property is sold, broker Kilbourne will receive a 6 percent commission.

Grant, an agent who works for Kilbourne, shows the property, holds open houses, and finds a buyer. Who gets the commission? Kilbourne is the broker so Kilbourne gets the fee at closing, $12,000 in this example. Kilbourne then turns around and pays some portion of the $12,000 commission to Grant for her work, according to whatever arrangement exists between them.

Under no condition can you pay the fee directly to Grant, because she is a salesperson and does not have the right to list or sell real estate on her own. In fact, Grant has no right to collect a fee or commission from anyone other than her broker.

SUBAGENCY AND COOPERATION

In our effort to find out who is who in real estate, we have come across principals, brokers, salespeople, agents, and agency.

Alas, the marketplace is often more complex.

With Kilbourne and Grant we had an "in-house" deal: broker Kilbourne listed the property, agent Grant brought in a buyer, and everything was done under the authority of Kilbourne's brokerage license.

But what happens if neither Kilbourne nor his agents sell the property? Suppose broker Kilbourne lists the property but broker Griffin has an interested buyer.

It's nice and wonderful that Griffin has a buyer, but a buyer is only part of the puzzle. Griffin needs property to show, but property can only be shown with the authority and consent of the owner or the owner's agent.

You can imagine that broker Kilbourne does not want Griffin showing the property unless he, Kilbourne, gets a part of the commission. You can also imagine that Kilbourne wants the property sold. The net result is that Kilbourne and Griffin make a deal: "Look, the place is listed for $200,000. Here's a form giving you permission to show the property as a subagent and stating that if you find a purchaser 'ready, willing, and able' to buy the property according to all listing requirements, you will receive a commission equal to 3 percent of the sales price."

Griffin now has the right to show the property, but he didn't get that right from the owner. Instead, Griffin obtained his authority to sell from

---

Tracing Traditional Agency

Owner (Principal)
↓
Listing Broker (Agent)→Salespeople
↓
Selling Broker (Subagent)→Salespeople

Tracing a Commission Split

Owner (Principal)
↓
Closing (Settlement)
↓
Commission ($12,000)
↓
Listing Broker ($6,000)↔Selling Broker ($6,000)
↓   ↓
Salesperson ($3,000)   Salesperson ($3,000)

Tracing Single Agency

Seller (Principal)   Buyer (Principal)
↓   ↓
Listing Broker   Buyer Broker

---

broker Kilbourne, the owner's agent. *Rather than being an agent, Griffin is a subagent.*

Now we have agency and subagency, and we also have fee splitting between the brokers. But what about salespeople? How do they fit into the agency/subagency system?

Imagine that agent Grant lists your property for $200,000 under the authority of broker Kilbourne. You agree to pay a 6 percent commission if the house sells. Agent Fenwick who works for broker Griffin finds a buyer. The property is sold for $200,000 and the total commission is 6 percent in this example, or $12,000. At closing brokers Kilbourne and Griffin each receive a commission check for $6,000. Broker Kilbourne then pays agent Grant a particular sum, say $3,000, while broker Griffin pays agent Fenwick $3,000.

In our deal with brokers Kilbourne and Griffin, we can see that the brokers split the commission and later paid their agents. We can also see that agency was first established between the seller and broker Kilbourne, and that subagency went from broker Kilbourne to broker Griffin. In effect, Kilbourne worked for the seller and Griffin worked for the seller. No one worked for the buyer, and while the brokers had a responsibility to treat the buyer fairly, they were obligated to get the best price and terms for their principal, the seller.

We can also see something else. As more brokers and agents became involved in the transaction, the commission amount remained the same but the slice earned by each broker and agent became smaller and smaller.

REFERRAL FEES

Between Grant, Kilbourne, Fenwick, and Griffin we saw that a single realty fee could be split four ways. But why stop with four? If we work at it, much of North America can be involved in the transaction.

Imagine that you live in California but know broker Ashton in Iowa. You tell Ashton that you want to sell and she introduces you to broker Kilbourne, someone she has worked with before.

The house is sold for $200,000. Agent Grant, who works for Kilbourne, handles the deal, and Fenwick—who works for broker Griffin—again finds the buyer. There is a 6 percent commission and at closing Kilbourne gets $6,000 and Griffin gets $6,000.

Kilbourne pays agent Grant $3,000 and Griffin pays $4,000 to Fenwick. In addition, Kilbourne pays $600 as a referral fee to broker Ashton in Iowa.

In addition to a referral fee related to listing the property, there can also be a listing fee for locating the buyer. And like the basic commission itself, it is entirely possible to have a referral fee divided by brokers and agents.

MLS SYSTEMS

Few terms in real estate are better known or less understood than the everyday expression "MLS."

Around the country there are some 1,500 multiple listing services (MLS) and of this number perhaps 1,400 are affiliated with local broker groups.

An MLS system is usually seen as a repository of local real estate information, a database where member brokers and their agents can quickly look up past sales and current listings. If Johnson wants a three-bedroom, two-bath house in the Foxborough subdivision, agent Carter can press a few buttons and quickly pinpoint every available home that meets Johnson's needs.

From the seller's perspective, an MLS has enormous value for several reasons.

First, it can be used to establish a realistic selling price. With an MLS, one can look at past sales and current offerings in a given neighborhood and have a good idea of local values, especially in subdivisions with large numbers of like properties.

Second, an MLS is a marketing tool. Place your home in an MLS and it will come up each time a member broker or agent seeks property that matches what you have in terms of price, location, size, and features. In effect, not only is a home marketed with an MLS, it is marketed at the point of sale when exposure will do the most good and has the greatest value.

Third, an MLS can be used to create agency and subagency.

To see how an MLS works—and to see why such systems have great value—imagine that your home has been listed by broker Newman for $194,999. The listing is an exclusive-right-to-sell arrangement and Newman is part of a local MLS.

Once the listing has been taken, Newman goes to his computer, calls the local MLS by modem, and adds your property to the system. As he goes through the listing form to code your property, he does more than describe your kitchen and lot size.

By listing your property in the system, Newman automatically makes a "blanket offer of subagency" to all member brokers who want to sell your property. Now you not only have Newman the agent, you also have an army of broker subagents. In turn, all the salespeople who work for member agents suddenly have authority to sell your home. In the case of some MLS systems, it means your home is available through thousands of individual brokers and salespeople.

No less important than the broad marketing base provided by the MLS, you have also created a business opportunity for all MLS members.

When Newman lists your property in the system, he not only wants to say that your home is terrific, *he also wants to make certain everyone understands that your home is a good business deal.* To be specific, he wants other brokers and salespeople in your town to realize that there's money to be made if they help sell your property.

Newman won't say what the full commission is between the two of you, and certainly the amount you agree to pay a broker is entirely negotiable, but Newman will announce in the MLS that a cooperative fee is available to the broker who finds a buyer, say a 3 percent co-op fee to other brokers.

BUYER BROKERS

In the first chapter we talked about the 1983 survey by the Federal Trade Commission documenting what many had long suspected: few consumers realize how the real estate marketing system works. According to the FTC, 74.2 percent of all homebuyers thought brokers and their agents represented them. Ten percent thought brokers worked for both buyers and sellers.

As a seller you could look at this survey and say, great, the brokerage system sure works for me. Buyers could look at the same information and decide, with equal accuracy, that someone ought to be protecting their interests, trying to get the best possible price and terms for them.

Brokers, also, have had discomfort with the seller orientation that has long been part of the real estate marketing system. How do you sell property to your best friend if you have an agency obligation to a seller, an obligation that commits you to get the best possible price and terms for the owner?

The result of buyer demand and broker concerns has led to a growing buyer-brokerage movement. In this situation we have a broker who acts as an agent for a buyer and has all the obligations that agency entails, which in this case means getting the best possible price and terms for his or her principal, the buyer.

Your goal, as a seller, is to market your home to anyone who comes up with the right package of dollars and benefits. Whether your purchaser has the assistance of a buyer broker, an attorney, or a soothsayer is beyond your control. But when buyers have professional assistance, beware: the bargaining process may not be as easy or direct as in the good old days.

Unlike "cooperation," where everyone works to help the seller, buyer brokers are marketplace adversaries. Their job is to assure that buyers pay as little as possible for your home and, indeed, success for a buyer broker often means financial pain for a seller.

Philosophically it can be argued that competition is good for the marketplace, but you're not a philosopher. You merely want to sell your home and to the extent that buyer brokers make the process more costly and less profitable, they are a hurdle to be overcome.

In terms of an MLS, it's obvious that a buyer broker cannot act as an owner's subagent because you—the seller—are not the principal of a buyer broker. But *a buyer broker can still use an MLS as a database* to find properties and as a guide to check prices for current listings and past sales.

In the same way that a selling broker wants to know how a home shapes up as a business deal, a buyer broker wants the same information. While a buyer representative cannot get a co-op fee, buyer brokers are typically paid from the money that would otherwise have gone to a selling broker. Here's how.

Suppose broker Crofton lists a home at $150,000 with a 6 percent commission. When entering the property into a local MLS, Crofton would probably offer a 3 percent co-op fee to a subagent who brings in a buyer.

But if the purchaser is represented by Grady, a buyer broker, there is no subagent. There is Crofton the listing broker and Grady the buyer broker. In an ideal world Crofton would receive a commission from his client, and Grady would be paid by the purchaser. But the world is less than perfect, so the deal usually works this way: with the seller's approval, the portion of the commission that could go to a co-op broker (3 percent in this example) is instead paid to Grady the buyer broker.

There's no rule that says listing broker Crofton must offer selling brokers (subagents) and buyer brokers (agents for a different principal) the same fee, and there is no rule that says a seller must permit such payments. But everyone is best served by making a deal, so it usually happens that a buyer broker is actually paid from funds set aside for a co-op sale.

DISCLOSURE

The matter of disclosure has always been a serious concern in real estate because of the possibility of accidental dual agency, but nothing much happened until the late 1980s and early 1990s when it was decided that uniform, mandated disclosure would be good for both consumers and professionals. As of the time this guide was written, more than 40 states had adopted disclosure regulations, and the rest are likely to follow.

Disclosure forms are important because they are one line of defense for brokers if a claim of dual agency is raised. They are also important because they can give buyers and sellers a better understanding of the real estate marketing system and who represents whom.

YOUR ROLE

You may look at your home and imagine that merely because you own it, live in it, fix it, and pay for it that somehow it is yours alone. In theory such thinking may be correct, but in practice your property is something more than a residence with your name on the door.

To the local government, your home is a source of tax revenue. The more expensive the better. If your home sells and you move away, that's great, too. As a homeseller you are potentially the best taxpayer in town—someone who pays big money to the local community, moves, and then uses someone else's roads and schools.

To members of the local bar, the sale of your property involves contracts, liens, deeds, and other paperwork that require the services of an attorney to create or understand.

Surveyors, on behalf of buyers and lenders, want to ensure that your property is where you think it is and that no other lots encroach on your land—or vice versa. Lenders see your property as security, a storehouse of economic value to protect their interests in case a debtor flies off to Rio without paying the mortgage.

Insurers see your home as a web of liabilities from which you and your buyer should be protected. Termite inspectors worry (hope?) that your home will be appetizing to a vast and hungry assortment of bugs. Decorators pray fervently that your buyer will require their services, while structural inspectors are available to explore such construction qualities as your home may enjoy. Or lack.

The hardware store favors lots of home sales, and the furniture company knows that people who buy homes also buy sofas and tables, so they're rooting for you to sell, please. Movers, of course, feel that no home sale is complete without their services, preferably services that require the crossing of several state borders.

And then, most visibly, we have real estate brokers and agents. Today we have traditional brokers, discount brokers, and flat-fee brokers to list and sell property. We have buyer brokers to represent purchasers, facilitators who represent no one, and dual agents who represent everyone.

Suddenly the house you own is interesting to many people. Your decision to sell or hold, to paint, refinance, subdivide, or rent involves many specialists and institutions, most of whom are more or less necessary in the homeselling process.

Alas, none work for free and therein lies the problem. Like you, professionals need to earn a living, and your marketplace choices—along with the decisions of other homesellers—will determine who has a good year and who doesn't.

Through it all there is one bottom-line test that should always be remembered: *your self-interest is at stake. If you don't protect it, if you don't look out for yourself, who will?*

Homeselling involves possibilities and perils. Your job is to maximize your profits and limit your risks to the extent possible, a process best begun by looking at the practical marketplace.

3
The Practical Marketplace

Having looked at how the real estate system operates, we can now address two questions of profound importance: how do you fit into the system and what is the best way to market your home?

Cutting through the malarkey, psycho-babble, puffery, baloney, and nonsense, home sales are dependent on several baseline issues:

- Is the property well located?
- Is the property well maintained?
- Is the property well priced?
- Is the property a good business deal for brokers and agents?
- Is the local economy stable, stagnant, declining, or expanding?
- Are interest rates reasonable?
- What zoning restrictions limit usage?
- Are there immediate local events that have an impact on the value and salability of your home? Are they positive or negative?
- Do you have "good and marketable title?" This expression generally means that an owner has title to a property, can sell, give, or will the property to another, and that in turn a buyer will have a sound ownership interest that can later be resold, given away, or willed.
- Is your home reasonably consistent with the neighborhood in terms of price, size, and condition?
- Is there a good marketing plan for your property, and is it well executed?

The baseline issues raise an important point: *Your goal is not just to place your home on the market. It's to make your property so attractive, so competitive, and so compelling that a sale with the price and terms you want is not in question.*

BROKER, SOME BROKER, OR NO BROKER?

The most basic marketing question faced by every owner is the issue of whether or not to use a broker, a matter that must be reviewed with care.

There are pros and cons to both self-selling and the use of brokers. Self-selling means that your time, labor, skills, and initiative are exchanged for a lower commission or no commission. If your home is worth $200,000 and you can save a 6 or 7 percent fee, there is an incentive worth as much as $12,000 to $14,000 to be successful.

But no one sells a home without cost. There is the value of your time, charges for signs and advertising, and there are underlying expenses as well. If you're not good at bargaining, the biggest expense may well be needless concessions buried in the form of a lesser price or weaker terms.

The brokerage option as well has pros and cons. One concern is that not all brokers and agents have equal ability and neither licensure nor MLS membership guarantees a sale. Another problem is that a broker, as your agent, can get you in trouble if he or she is poorly trained or incompetent. And the most visible issue, of course, is that brokerage services cost money.

Hiring a broker, however, is not without benefits. Someone else has a big financial incentive to make your deal work. Because they are not emotionally attached to the property, brokers and agents can give advice that is not influenced by sentimental concerns.

Brokers, as well, sell homes for a living. It's what they do. By virtue of training, experience, and access to professional tools, they *should* be able to do a superior job.

Until the 1980s, the usual options for homesellers were to either go the Fizzbo route or leave the sale in the hands of a broker. Now a third option has emerged, arrangements where owners do some of the work and brokers do a share as well. The attraction of such deals is that costs are lower and owners can find help in those areas where they are weak or need professional advice. The problem in some cases is that a fee may be earned, regardless of whether or not the property is sold.

Reviewing today's options, these are the choices available in most communities.

Traditional Brokerage. For the past 75 years, and probably longer, traditional brokerage has been used to market most homes. With traditional brokerage the broker handles all aspects of the sale, including pricing (with the owner's approval), showing, advertising, working with other brokers, negotiating, and managing transaction details. A single fee related to the ultimate sale price, say 6 or 7 percent, is due and payable when the terms of a listing are met.

Traditional brokerage is commonly an all-or-nothing deal. The broker provides a given bundle of services and receives a particular fee. With traditional brokerage there is usually:

- No owner participation
- Agency created with an exclusive listing
- The use of one or more MLS systems

The idea of traditional brokerage is to take all the problems and issues associated with a home sale, handle them, and finish the process at closing when the owner receives a check. Traditional brokerage works well for those owners who want as little hassle as possible when it comes time to sell their property.

Discount Brokerage. Traditional brokerage envisions the purchase of a given bundle of services for a given fee, but a discount broker has a somewhat different approach.

A discount broker looks at the costs of doing business and sees that a large portion of his or her professional time is spent in the competition for listings with other brokers who are likely to charge the same fees, offer the same services, use the same forms, belong to the same MLS, and employ the same marketing strategies.

In marketing this situation is known as "clutter," meaning that no competitor stands out. A consumer can chose broker Smith or broker Jones and it makes no difference because the costs and services are the same. Discount brokers, to earn distinction, offer a traditional package of services but at a somewhat lower fee.

How can discount brokers charge less? Easy. Because they have a distinct advantage marketing their services, they spend less professional time hunting for listings. Sellers come to discounters. In effect, the discount is a marketing tool designed to bring in additional brokerage business.

Not all discounters offer a full bundle of services, however. If a discount deal looks interesting, be certain to compare services with a traditional broker to see what you're getting and what may be missing. If a service or benefit is missing, that may be okay in exchange for a lower fee, depending on what you need and want.

What's not okay when working with a discounter is a fee split that fails to lure other brokers to your property.

Suppose that traditional brokers in your area routinely receive a 6 percent fee for marketing homes. Suppose as well that Discount Dave offers to sell your property with a 4 percent fee. The lower fee looks better from the seller's viewpoint, but what about other brokers?

A large proportion of all residential sales are co-op deals that involve

---

Are Fees Negotiable?

One of the most contentious issues in real estate is the matter of fees. So there should be no confusion about the subject, it must be said that fees are absolutely negotiable, they are not set by law, there is no such thing as a "standard" commission, and no group or governmental agency sets fees.

In the past the regulatory bodies that were supposed to oversee the industry "to protect the public interest" did little to encourage price competition. In the District of Columbia, the *Real Estate and Business Chance Manual* published by the local real estate commission in the 1960s stated that a broker "should respect the schedule of fees established by custom in his community," advice not to be ignored when the sponsoring body has the right to suspend or revoke licenses.

Today matters are different. Real estate commissions are absolutely negotiable. This does *not* mean that a broker must accept whatever price you think is fair, but it does mean that brokers—like lawyers, doctors, engineers, architects, and other professionals—cannot work together to establish a uniform cost for their services.

Oddly enough, while the real estate industry has done much to become more competitive, the federal agency that oversees housing matters is still behind the times.

A 1990 homebuyer booklet from the Department of Housing and Urban Development (HUD), "A Home of Your Own: Helpful Advice from HUD on Choosing, Buying, and Enjoying a Home," tells readers that if you buy a HUD property, "HUD will pay your real estate broker's commission—up to the standard 6 percent of the sales price."

A few blocks away from HUD headquarters in Washington, at the Justice Department where the Sherman Anti-Trust Act is administered, you can bet that if a real estate broker told consumers there was a "standard 6 percent" commission, price-fixing indictments would be finished by the next morning.

And in case you think the HUD statement is a typo of some sort, consider this: the 6 percent "standard" appears twice, once on page 9 and again on page 30.

fee splitting. Seen another way, if a house is not a good co-op deal, you lose part of the market.

If I'm a broker and I have buyers in hand, I'll want to find a home for my prospects. I'll also want to find a home that represents a good deal for me.

If I see that Discount Dave has a nice house for sale, I'll certainly show it to my prospects, the theory being that a sale is better than no sale. But if Dave is getting a 4 percent commission, and if Dave is paying a 2 percent co-op fee, his listing is a last resort because in a market where brokers often list homes at 6 percent, 3 percent co-op fees will be common.

Being tainted with a strong sense of self-interest, I will emphasize the properties that meet the needs of my prospects *and* that offer the highest co-op fees. Discount Dave, while he's surely a nice fellow, needs to pay me more—at least as much as other brokers—if he wants my attention.

Can Discount Dave adjust his fees so that he gets more co-op action? Sure. Dave can charge his 4 percent fee, but in a 6 percent market he must be willing to pay a 3 percent co-op fee so that his listings can compete with other properties.

As a seller you want access to co-op brokers because the more brokers that come to your property, the greater your chances for a sale. Reduce the co-op fee and your home becomes less attractive as a business deal.

So is it okay to use a discounter? If the co-op split is appropriate for your local market, discounters can be attractive.

Flat-Fee Brokers. While discount brokers compete with traditionalists by offering a reduced fee, flat-fee brokers take the bundle of services offered by traditional brokers and break it apart. Just pick and choose the services you want, pay for what you get, and forget the rest. For instance, a flat-fee broker may have separate charges to erect a sign, hold an open house, negotiate with a purchaser, work on closing issues, advertise, find financing for the purchaser, etc.

A flat-fee broker may charge just a few dollars or maybe nothing to place your home in the local MLS, but here again we come to the issue of co-op fees.

Placing a home in the MLS will have little value without an attractive co-op fee. To induce other brokers to show their properties, flat-fee brokers must be able to offer competitive co-op fees, and that means an additional charge to cover such a cost in the event of a co-op sale.

There is an enormous amount of logic to the flat-fee approach, but it's clearly not for everyone. Sellers, for example, commonly hold their own open houses when working with flat-fee firms. That's fine if you're comfortable showing a house and if you can use the showing process to bargain and negotiate, but not everyone is good at sales.

Moreover, it should be said that flat-fee brokers are not necessarily cheap. Add the flat fee to a co-op charge if the home is sold through another broker, and it is possible for savings to be minimal or nonexistent.

SELF-LISTING

While there is no shortage of brokers who would welcome the opportunity to sell your home, as a matter of self-interest every owner–seller should consider the option of self-selling.

Since nearly 20 percent of all existing home sales involve self-selling, it is fairly obvious that this subject cannot be overlooked, nor should it be. Marketing a home is a costly venture and if self-selling reduces that expense or offers other benefits, then why not see if the Fizzbo route makes sense for you?

If you elect to act as a self-seller you will have to price your property, market it, show it, negotiate, work with a broker or attorney who can provide professional advice on an hourly basis, offer financing hints and suggestions to your buyer, participate in closing, and do all the things it takes to make a deal work.

In exchange for your labors you may be able to save an amount equal to much or all of the commission.

What you won't be able to do is to sell your home for "free." It costs money to advertise and hire professional help, and it takes time to market a home. If you value your time, then the expense of self-selling can be steep in periods when real estate sales are slow.

As a self-seller you can advertise in the newspapers, hold open houses, show the property by appointment, and use signs and handouts. You won't get access to the local MLS or relocation services, and it is probable that local real estate photo guides will not accept your ad.

Despite these barriers, many people do sell their own houses. The ones most likely to succeed study the market with care, prepare their properties, and use lawyers and brokers as consultants paid on an hourly basis.

Can self-selling work for you? One choice is to try self-selling for a while and then switch to a broker if you don't find success. A second option is to be less than pure and work with a broker to fill in those areas where your skills are limited.

Why Self-Sellers Sell

According to the National Association of Realtors, Fizzbos enter the market-place for a variety of reasons. Here, in order, are the results of a national survey showing why owners elect to sell their own homes.

Reason	Percentage
Did not want to pay a commission or fee	46
Did not want to deal with a broker or agent	12
Broker was unable to sell home	11
Sold to friend or neighbor	8
Sold to family member	7
Buyer contacted seller directly	7
Had a real estate license	4
Other	4
Sold to a homebuying company	1
Could not find a broker	°

°Less than 1 percent.

(Source: *The Homebuying and Selling Process*, 1991, National Association of Realtors. See Table 5.14.)

A third choice—one used by some self-sellers—is to use self-selling as a negotiating tool to gain a better deal with brokers.

Suppose that Imhoff is marketing his property as a self-seller when broker Taylor stops by. Taylor says he has a possible buyer and would like a twenty-four-hour exclusive listing to show the property.

Imhoff says that an open listing is certainly possible, at which point Taylor whips out a nicely printed form and fills in the blanks. One of those blanks shows the broker's commission, an amount Taylor calculates at 6 percent.

Imhoff, however, is not so sure. After all, it is seller Imhoff who is advertising the house, holding it open, negotiating, and doing the broker's work. You could say that Imhoff has really listed his own house, and since he is not working for another for a fee, he needs no license.

Imhoff, knowing how the system works, makes this offer to Taylor: An open listing with a 3 percent commission, the same amount that Taylor would get with most other co-op deals.

Now Taylor has a problem. If the buyer sees the house and it's not listed, Taylor will not get a commission. If he takes 3 percent, that's the same deal he might receive from a listing broker. Taylor sees that he can't get 6 percent, but maybe he can do better than 3 percent. He tells Imhoff he'll take the open listing if the seller will pay 4 percent. Does Imhoff accept the deal? In a hot market with lots of buyers, Imhoff sticks to 3 percent. But in a market that favors buyers, Imhoff would be foolish to pass up Taylor's offer.

If the Imhoff property sells for $175,000 and the commission is reduced by 2 percent, then at the end of the deal Imhoff has an additional $3,500 in his pocket. If Imhoff can reduce the marketing bill by 3 percent of the sales price, then he is ahead by $5,250.

In addition to saving money, Imhoff has done something else: he has *used Fizzbo status as a lever to get a better commission rate*. Whether the Imhoffs of the world really want to be self-sellers, or whether they use self-selling merely as a ploy to negotiate with brokers, the bottom line is more bargaining power in the marketplace.

WHEN YOU NEED A BROKER

There is an oddity with real estate sales that shows up constantly. When markets are slow, sellers want to maximize profits and often think that the best way to magnify sale results is to cut brokers out of the deal. But slow markets are exactly when broker services are most likely to benefit owners.

When markets are scorching and buyers line up outside the door, owner reactions are often different. Why worry about brokerage fees when prices are going up daily? There's more than enough to pay a broker and still come out far ahead. The truth, of course, is that hot markets are hot for both brokers and self-sellers, and are thus the best time to be a Fizzbo.

While owners should at least study self-selling, any consideration of Fizzbo status should be tempered with the thought that selling your own home is not for everyone.

1) If you're not sales-oriented, then self-selling is a poor marketing choice. It takes a certain persona and moxie to be in sales, and not everyone has such skills.

2) If you're moving out of the area, you'll need a broker. Long-distance self-selling is a miserable idea because there is no way to show the property if a buyer suddenly shows up at the front door.

3) If you're short on cash it can pay to hire a broker. Yes, you'll pay a

fee for the broker's services—but you'll only pay if the property sells. Meanwhile, it is the broker who pays for advertising, signs, and other marketing costs.

4) Self-selling is not a good choice when the market is slow. There are few buyers at such times, so the worth and importance of brokerage services increases.

5) If your home is expensive it will pay to get a broker. Self-selling and million-dollar homes are somehow incongruous. If you have a mansion, the probability is that the value of your time is maximized doing other things.

6) If you have a busy schedule and a hectic lifestyle that will not allow you to drop everything to show the house, then the use of a broker is probably a good idea.

4
How to Bargain with a Broker

The relationship between owner and broker is that of principal and agent—but only *after* a listing agreement has been signed. Before you take on a broker and make him or her your agent, that person has an absolute right to seek the biggest possible commission and the best terms. You—as a consumer—have an equally absolute right to seek the best deal you can get and to hold down brokerage fees to the barest minimum.

A careful look at listing arrangements shows that far more is at stake in addition to such visible issues as format and fees. If we review the fine print with care, we can perfect a listing agreement so that instead of being a flawless pro-broker document, the wording reflects a more balanced arrangement.

What's in a listing agreement? What's left out? Precise answers will depend on where you live and the type of listing involved. That said, here's a list of major issues to consider when hiring a broker.

MONEY

Real estate fees are entirely negotiable and as a seller you want to assure that two central fee issues are addressed.

First, how much is the commission?

Second, in the event of a co-op sale or a deal with a buyer broker, how is the commission divided?

Commissions are typically expressed as a percentage of the selling prices (say 6 percent of the sales price), and in a co-op situation or where a buyer broker is involved, fees are usually split 50/50.

Marketplace realities mean that if you use a broker you must structure the fee so that co-op brokers and buyer brokers will find your home attractive. In English, this means you'll need a co-op fee of 3 percent or better in a community where 6 percent commissions are common.

Suppose you live in a community—let's call it Edenview—where homes are typically sold with a 6 percent realty fee. In Edenview, as well, 3-percent co-op fees are widely available. Let's also imagine that your home has a market value of $200,000, so a 6 percent commission is worth $12,000.

A traditional deal is fine, but there is no rule which says fees must be structured in only one method. Instead of a percentage deal, you could have a given fee, say $5,000 or whatever, regardless of the sale price.

In fact, rather than a single fee based on the selling price, it's possible to have an array of commissions, percentages, and fees depending on your needs and the local market.

Dual Fee. In this scenario you list your home with broker Ardsdale so that one of two commissions are available. If the home is sold cooperatively or with a buyer broker, then you'll pay a 6 percent fee: 3 percent to the listing broker and 3 percent for a co-op commission. If the property is both listed and sold by Ardsdale, then there is no co-op fee involved and the total payment to Ardsdale will be 4 percent.

> Example 1: Ardsdale lists your home for $200,000 and broker Sanchez brings in a buyer. The commission is 6 percent of $200,000, or $12,000. Both Ardsdale and Sanchez receive $6,000 at closing.

> Example 2: Ardsdale lists and sells your home for $200,000 and receives a commission worth 4 percent, or $8,000 in this illustration.

The dual-fee approach has little downside for a broker and offers potential savings for an owner. All told, not a bad accommodation for either side.

Uneven Split. With an uneven split there can be two possible commission levels: say 5 percent if the deal is a co-op sale and 4 percent if the property is listed and sold by a single broker.

> Example 3: Your property is listed at $200,000 with an uneven split arrangement by broker Rokerby. Rokerby finds a buyer and receives a 4 percent commission, $8,000 in this example.

Example 4: Broker Rokerby lists your home for $200,000 and broker Reese finds a buyer. At closing Rokerby gets 2 percent ($4,000) and Reese receives 3 percent ($6,000), a total of 5 percent ($10,000).

The uneven-split approach effectively encourages brokers to sell the homes they list, thus eliminating the need to pay a co-op broker or a buyer broker. While it's true that 4 percent to list and sell a home is less than the 6 percent brokers might otherwise receive in this example, it's also true that the property represents a business opportunity for the broker where he or she can actually make more money than in a co-op deal.

Declining Balance. Commissions today are generally proportional to a property's sale price, perhaps 6 percent of a $100,000 sale or 6 percent of a $300,000 deal. However, there is no rule that says commissions must be consistent regardless of price. With the declining-balance plan you might pay several rates, depending on the ultimate sale price.

Example 5: You list your home with broker Donaldson for $200,000. Donaldson lists and sells the property. She receives a commission equal to 6 percent of the first $100,000 and 5 percent of everything above $100,000.

Example 6: Donaldson lists the property for $200,0000 and broker Stern finds a buyer. The commission, which is split evenly between the brokers, amounts to 6 percent of the first $100,000 and 5 percent of the balance.

If the declining-balance format is used, it's possible for the co-op split to be less than the amount a selling broker or buyer broker might otherwise receive with a traditional deal. For this reason, a declining balance is best used when expensive homes are being sold because even though the percentage is marginally lower than other co-op deals, the absolute number of dollars involved is significant. For example, if the Conklin home sells for $850,000 with a 6 percent commission on the first $500,000 and a 4 percent fee on everything above $500,000, then the payment amounts to $44,000 ($500,000 × 6 percent + $350,000 × 4 percent). There are not too many people who would turn down a $22,000 co-op fee.

Merit Commission, I. In a down market, or to reach a certain sale price, it can make sense to create a better business deal for brokers. In this case, rather than lowering the commission, the brokerage fee is raised.

Example 7: You want to sell your home for $200,000 but times are tough. Most homes in your community carry 6 percent realty commissions, which means that a typical co-op fee is 3 percent. You list your home at 6.5 percent, with the understanding that the co-op fee is to be set at 3.5 percent.

Merit Commission, II. You want to move your home in a tough market, so you simply offer a bigger commission to everyone.

Example 8: In a market where many homes are listed at 6 percent, you offer 7 percent. In the event of a co-op sale, both the listing broker and the selling broker each receive 3.5 percent of the sales price.

Straight Discount. Instead of paying 6 percent you pay a lesser figure. Discounted deals can work, but beware: a straight discount may reduce your ability to attract selling brokers and buyer representatives. For instance, if a discounter offers a 2 percent co-op fee in a market where 3 percent co-op deals are common, the smaller fee will not be competitive to selling brokers and buyer brokers.

Net Commission. A truly bad idea, one banned in many states. With a net commission you seek a certain sales price and the broker gets everything higher.

The problem with a net commission is that it provides an opportunity for unscrupulous brokers to dupe unsophisticated sellers. With net commissions an owner is likely to rely on the broker for pricing information and advice. The broker can then suggest a price far below the property's real worth, sell it for a top price, and pocket the difference. For instance, if the Collins property has a market value of $200,000, but Collins thinks the property is only worth $150,000, broker Hastings can (if legal) suggest a $150,000 sale price and a net listing. If the property then sells for $200,000, Hastings will receive a $50,000 fee.

Consultant Fee. In this situation you hire a broker on a project or hourly basis to provide advice and information. A broker in a major metropolitan area, for example, might charge $100 per hour. If you subsequently list the property with the consulting broker, any fees paid to the broker would be deducted from a sales commission if the property is sold.

This arrangement has several attractions for both sellers and brokers. For owners, it provides the information base you may want if you intend to act as a self-seller. Representation need not be involved in a consulting relationship, so the problem of agency liability is removed.

For the broker, there is a fee whether or not the property is sold. If the owner elects to list the property, the consulting broker will already have a working relationship with the owner. In addition, it makes financial sense for an owner to list with the consulting broker because some or all consulting fees can be a credit to the owner in the event of a sale.

> Example 9: You hire broker Douglas as a consultant and agree to pay $100 an hour. Over several weeks Douglas puts in seven hours. After having the home on the market for several weeks, you list with broker Douglas. He sells the property for $200,000 and receives a 6 percent commission. At closing, Douglas receives a $12,000 fee less a $700 credit, or a balance due of $11,300.

Flat Fee. In this scenario you want to be a self-seller but you need some help. Broker Burns agrees to provide signs ($125), marketing advice ($250), advertising ($250), and negotiating assistance ($300). You decline the opportunity to have Burns hold open houses, negotiate with a purchaser, or locate financing.

Flat-fee deals can work and, in certain cases, they can be money savers because you're trading owner labor for a reduced brokerage fee. But if co-op deals with other brokers are important, then be careful to compare flat-fee charges with the commissions sought by other brokers.

For instance, if broker Reynolds charges $1,800 to market your home for a given bundle of services plus 3 percent of the sale price in the event of a co-op sale, then the cost to market a $150,000 property will be $6,300 if another broker brings in a buyer or a buyer broker is involved in the sale.

In effect, the proper comparison in this case between a broker charging 6 percent and a flat-fee broker is not $9,000 versus $1,800, it's $9,000 measured against $6,300. While a $2,700 difference is significant, it must be measured against the services *not* provided by the flat-fee broker.

If the property is sold directly, however, if no co-op fee is involved and no buyer broker is part of the sale, then the $1,800 flat fee becomes very enticing. The catch, of course, is that no one knows in advance how the property will be sold, and thus the final marketing fee is uncertain.

LISTING ISSUES

Money is not a minor issue and it's appropriate to evaluate commission choices with care. But fees are not the only concerns with a real estate listing; other matters must also be addressed if you are to have a good deal with a broker.

Address. The listing form will show both the street address (4320 Valleyview Road) and the legal description (Lot 4, Block 6, of Wilton's Subdivision). Both addresses are used to assure that the property being sold is the same property described in local property records. In addition, by placing the formal legal description on the listing, it means that co-op brokers and buyer brokers need not look up such information when making an offer.

Adjustments. As part of the deal, you agree to make adjustments at closing. For example, if there are unpaid property taxes, then money from the sale will be used to pay such liens.

Advertising. State regulations generally prohibit real estate advertising without an owner's permission. The result is that listing agreements can create permission for a broker to advertise the property, erect a sign, use photos of the property, and enter the home into a local MLS because the use of an MLS can be viewed as a form of promotion.

Advertising is important to a broker because it can "introduce" prospects to the property and such introductions can then lead to a fee.

Backup Offers. Once a buyer has been found, many sellers regard the property as "sold." It isn't. The deal can fall through for a number of reasons—a poor structural inspection, bad credit, insufficient income, etc. A listing agreement may provide that once an offer has been accepted, the broker is no longer obligated to market the property.

Many sellers will not agree to this clause, the view being that a deal is only done when a check is received at closing. In effect, by saying they will consider backup offers, owners are telling brokers to continue marketing even after an offer has been received and accepted.

Bias. As a matter of public policy, when you list your home with a broker you are obligated to make the property available to everyone. A broker cannot accept a listing where there is any suggestion that one group or another should be excluded from the marketing process.

Broker's Job. This clause says the broker's job is to "effect" the sale of the home. It also says the broker is not responsible for theft, damage, repairs, or management of the property.

In addition, many forms point out that since the broker's job is to find a "ready, willing, and able" buyer, the broker's obligations end once a buyer has been found. In practice, since brokers want the deal to go to closing, they typically assist with the many details that must be cleaned up once a buyer has been located.

Cash. An interesting clause in some listing forms requires the seller to bring enough cash to closing to assure that all liens are paid off and the broker's commission is paid. Not much of an issue—unless you are selling at a loss.

Timing. A fee will be due and payable when a "ready, willing, and able" buyer is found who meets the exact terms of the listing agreement.

In this clause sellers typically agree to pay the commission, but the broker agrees to defer payment until closing. The important point is that if a commission is earned, due, and payable, it is owed to the broker even if there is no closing.

Contract Form. Along with a listing you should receive a copy of the standardized form contract used by the broker. *Review this document with care, or have it reviewed by an attorney.* Buried in the fine print are a host of concessions and understandings that you may or may not want to make.

It may well be that you will want to use the broker's form because such documents tend to be pro-seller. That said, one must ask if agreeing to use a given form also constitutes an agreement to the terms and conditions in the form. Sellers sometimes change the listing language to say that the offer form must be satisfactory to them.

Cooperation. Exclusive and exclusive-right-to-sell agreements will include permission for a broker to market the property on a cooperative basis. In addition, a growing number of listing forms will also provide for a payment to a buyer broker if one is involved in the transaction.

As a seller, you want cooperation. And while it may be galling, you also want to make a payment available to buyer brokers. Why? Because buyer brokers represent purchasers and you need buyers to make the deal work.

Exclusivity. We know that brokers greatly prefer exclusive deals, but what happens if you've been acting as a self-seller and have the names of several prospects? Unless there is a clause to the contrary in an exclusive-right-to-sell agreement, you may owe a commission if one of your buyers purchases during the listing period.

There's no rule, however, that says an exclusive-right-to-sell agreement cannot be modified with appropriate language. Suppose buyers Donaldson, Krammer, and Yorkel saw your property when you held an open house as a self-seller. A listing agreement can be modified so that it will apply to all buyers *except* Donaldson, Krammer, and Yorkel.

Deposit. As a seller, you want the biggest possible deposit so that a buyer will either stick with the deal or cover your costs and expenses if he or she does not go through with the sale. As a practical matter you may not be able to get a huge deposit, but for purposes of a listing agreement you should ask for a hefty sum, say 5 to 10 percent of the sale price.

Entire Agreement. In the course of a listing presentation, a broker may offer a variety of plans and proposals. In the listing, however, there is generally language that says only those items outlined in the listing agreement count. Viewed another way, oral promises not included in the agreement are worthless.

Because of clauses that limit the broker's obligations to those items written into the listing contract, it can make sense to amend the agreement so that the broker's marketing plan is "attached to and made a part of" the listing compact.

Environmental Issues. Over the past several years, special environmental concerns such as radon, hazardous materials, and electromagnetic fields have become increasingly important to purchasers. More buyers, for example, now seek radon tests when buying a home despite the fact that such tests are notoriously inaccurate and a substantial body of scientific opinion questions whether any homeowner, anywhere, has ever gotten cancer from household radon emissions.

Listing forms increasingly ask sellers to certify that their homes do not contain excess amounts of radon or other environmental hazards. As a seller, such clauses should be a matter of concern because you are unlikely to have the technical expertise to make such assertions and, also, because not everyone defines environmental hazards the same way.

Given such unclear standards, many sellers handle environmental issues by allowing buyers a period of several days to test the home at their (the purchasers) expense and with an inspector of their choice. If the home is not "satisfactory," then the deal is off and the buyer's deposit is returned in full.

Fixtures. When you sell a home it is generally understood that you are also selling those parts of the house that are attached and intended to be a

Broker Disputes

Among the millions of deals between sellers and brokers, a small percentage lead to fights and disputes. In the event sparring breaks out, here are steps to take.

First, speak with the agent and explain why you are dissatisfied. It may be that there has been miscommunication or inadequate contact; whatever the problem, the agent should make a point of hearing your concerns.

Second, if you can't make progress with the agent, speak with the agent's broker or office manager and explain the problem.

Sellers in the dispute process have substantial leverage. A real estate brokerage is a local business and the last thing any broker wants is an argument with someone in the community, particularly someone with many friends and acquaintances.

If you have a situation where you no longer want to continue the listing, then matters are somewhat different.

A listing agreement is a contract that must be honored by both sellers and brokers. At the same time, many brokers make a practice of canceling listings when an owner is dissatisfied even if time remains to market the home. Other brokers will agree to terminate a listing in advance if a seller pays the broker's costs to service the property, expenses such as advertising, printing, MLS fees, etc.

Given a choice, no broker wants to feud with an owner. If you have a legitimate gripe, speak up and assert your interests. Most brokers, most of the time, will want to work with you to resolve the matter.

If communication with a broker does not work, contact the local real estate association and ask if they can handle a dispute. If yes, ask how problems are resolved. Professional associations, by their nature, do not want their industry sullied, and will try to help both sides.

As a last resort, *for the most serious disputes only*, contact the state real estate commission by phone, explain your problem (without naming names, for the moment), and ask how to proceed with a complaint. Next, contact the broker and ask if the matter should be pursued with the real estate commission, an exalted body with the authority to take away licenses, set fines, and refer matters to the attorney general's office. If a broker has behaved badly it will make great sense to settle the matter privately.

part of the home. These so-called "fixtures" remain with the property and convey to the new owner at closing. The usual example concerns microwave ovens. The microwave that is built in and attached to the house is a fixture, while the microwave that sits on a counter is not built in, not permanently attached, and not intended to go with the property.

Instead of being a fixture, the countertop microwave oven is "personalty."

A broker, however, has no right to sell something unless the seller gives permission. A listing will typically ask the seller to declare that certain items are fixtures and that the broker can include them in the sale price. Fixtures can include plumbing and lighting fixtures, furnaces, central air conditioning systems, cornices, curtain rods, the kitchen stove, awnings, screens, storm doors, and trees and shrubs.

As a seller you can make something a fixture by saying it is included in the sale. You can also make something into personalty by saying that it's not part of the deal.

As a bargaining ploy, you may want to say that certain items—such as clothes washers and dryers—are personalty even if you don't want them. Then, if a low offer comes in, you can always say, "Well, if you would raise your offer by $2,000 (or whatever) I'll accept the deal and even throw in the washer and dryer."

Format. Is the listing an open arrangement, an exclusive agency contract, or an exclusive-right-to-sell agreement? Is there a requirement to place the property in a local MLS?

Sellers should review proposed agreements with care. In particular, read the fine print. Make certain you understand the type of listing being sought and only agree to the format that best meets your needs. Make sure as well that the headline on the form agrees with the content. A listing that says "Standard Listing Form" or whatever at the top of the page may well obligate you to an "exclusive-right-to-sell" agreement in the fine print.

Loan Placement Fees (Points). A broker will often want you to state, as part of the listing, the number of points you are willing to pay as part of the deal. The listing agreement may also say that regardless of whatever number you choose, your obligation to pay points can rise or fall, depending on "changes" in the money market. Since money-market rates change daily, owners who agree to such terms essentially agree to pay whatever the market requires, whether one point or ten.

Savvy sellers often strike point requirements from the listing for three reasons. First, if you pay a point, you have discounted the sale price of your property. Second, if you offer to pay points when you list the property, you have made a concession without even seeing what a buyer is willing to offer. Third, the "reasonable change" language of many listing forms essentially commits you to pay whatever points a lender might want.

Lockboxes. When a home is entered into an MLS or listed by a large company, it is possible that many agents will want access to the property, access that may include times when neither your nor your broker is available. Since you want to maximize access to the property, it makes sense to have a lockbox that brokers can use to enter the property when you are not home.

For listing purposes a broker will want your authority to use a lockbox and to assure that he or she is not liable in the event of theft or damage to the property by someone who uses the lockbox—a problem that is not common but has happened.

The official protocol in real estate is that even with a lockbox, no one is supposed to enter the property without permission of the broker or owner. In practice, homes are routinely entered because an agent is in the car with a buyer, they're in front of the house, and neither the listing broker nor the owner is available.

Lockboxes should be used, when possible, but with precautions. One protection is to remove lockboxes when you are home, thus preserving your privacy. A second protection is to put away valuables when a home is listed.

Liens. You agree in the listing to pay off all existing loans and obligations secured by the property, except when such obligations are to be taken over by the purchaser. For example, you must pay off the old $75,000 first trust except if the buyer is to assume the loan

Modification. To earn a commission, a broker must completely satisfy every aspect of a listing agreement, but the marketplace is not always predictable and listing forms commonly contain an interesting stipulation: the broker is entitled to a fee if you accept the listing terms *or* a modification of the listing requirements. If you list a property at $195,000 and the broker brings in a buyer at $189,900, then the broker will earn a commission if you accept the lower figure. This clause is entirely practical and reasonable because it only takes effect if you accept an offer.

Papers. If you are selling a condominium, co-op, or planned unit development (PUD), then you are selling property with fewer rights than "fee-simple" real estate. To show what rights are for sale, and what rights are not for sale, you must provide appropriate documents for the buyer, such as declarations, covenants, co-op records, budgets, etc.

The broker wants a copy of these papers because there may be a review period associated with your property. For instance, a buyer in your state may have a three-day period to review condo documents, a period that only begins when the proper paperwork is delivered to the purchaser. During this review period, if the papers are not satisfactory to the buyer then the deal can be called off without the purchaser losing his or her deposit.

A clause that requires sellers to have appropriate papers in hand is good for everyone because ultimately such papers will be required to close the deal.

Price. The gross dollar amount you want for your property before deductions.

Protection Period. A listing has a given term, say 60 or 90 days, but what happens if a home is shown during the listing period but the purchaser buys after the listing expires?

This is a tricky question. Understandably, the broker wants to be paid for his or her work, while at the same time a protection period should not be too broad.

First, a protection period should be reasonable: 30 days rather than six months.

Second, the protection period should end automatically if the home is listed with another broker. Beware of forms where the protection period ends only if the property is listed with a local MLS member. Such language can restrict your choices after the listing expires.

Receipt. A listing will state, directly above the signature block, that a copy of the agreement has been received by the owner.

"Sale." While the goal of a broker is to sell a home, other situations may arise that take the place of an outright purchase. For this reason a commission is commonly due and payable in the event of a trade or exchange.

Settlement Costs. You may find that the buyers in your area have the right to select the closing provider, not a major issue since settlement must follow all contract terms. Some listings, however, contain a clause where sellers agree to pay "reasonable" closing costs as part of the deal. Many sellers limit their closing-cost obligations to a specific amount because they are concerned that the buyer may pick the most expensive closing agent in town.

Sewer and Water. In many states, water and sewage service is provided by the local government. Not surprisingly, governments that own water plants have decided that unpaid bills are a lien against your property. If you pay your bills there is no problem, but it is unlikely that the water meter was read five minutes before closing. Since you are selling your home without liens, and since an unpaid water bill is a lien, many listing forms state that you will agree to create an escrow account at closing to pay off any outstanding bills for showers and baths.

Smoke Detectors. In a growing number of communities, a home cannot be sold without smoke detectors. A listing may point out that smoke detectors are required, the broker's way of saying that you must install them prior to closing.

Take-Back Financing. More complex listing forms ask if you will "take back" financing from a buyer; that is, if you will loan some of the money required to make the deal.

Whether you want to take back financing or not, you must be careful with this clause. A listing form that says you will "consider" seller financing is acceptable, but a form that *obligates* you to take back a loan is not justifiable because you have no idea at the time of listing who will buy the property, what they earn, or if they pay their bills. Thus the listing is too early in the marketing process to make a financing commitment.

Term. Aside from format and the commission, one of the most crucial issues to brokers—and to sellers—is the listing term. For brokers, the goal is to have the longest possible listing because more time equals more opportunities to find a purchaser.

From the seller's perspective, the view is somewhat different. You want the broker to have enough time to market the property and find success, but you also know that some brokers promise diamonds but deliver glass.

One defense is a reasonable listing term. Many sellers work the term issue this way: they explain to the broker that they will list the property for 60 days, 90 days, or whatever is appropriate, and they will renew the listing if the broker follows through on promises to advertise, hold open houses, conduct mailings, etc.

Termite Inspection. A listing may state that as a seller you will pay for a termite inspection in a deal financed with a VA mortgage; otherwise the buyer will pay for an inspection.

Some forms go further and say that you will pay for treatment if an infestation exists, a requirement that makes sense. Less sensible is form language without a cap on repair costs. For instance, if you agree to pay "reasonable" termite damage repairs you may be making a commitment to pay thousands of dollars in fix-up costs.

Transfer Taxes. Local taxes are a big expense and some listing agreements attempt to pre-negotiate the issue by saying that unless otherwise agreed in the sales contract, you will pay half of all transfer taxes—perhaps thousands of dollars.

The question is, why should you agree to pay anything before an offer is on the table? Many sellers mark out such language and agree to consider the issue when an offer is received.

Warranty. The broker does not want responsibility for the property's condition and to every extent possible will want to show that all information regarding the house came from you. One approach is to have a clause in the listing that says you warrant all listing information.

A second—and increasingly common—technique is to use a "housing information questionnaire" that is attached and made a part of both the listing agreement and the sales contract.

The idea behind the questionnaire is to have the seller describe the property's condition through a series of questions and checklists. This seems logical and reasonable, until the point is raised that most people do not have the technical skills, training, or experience to evaluate their own homes.

If someone asks, "Is the roof leaking?" do you have an answer? Have you been in the attic—every part of the attic—during a storm? Is the question absolute, or is it meant to be a relative question? That is, if a tenth of an ounce of water gets into the attic each decade, then within the meaning of the question does the roof leak?

Questionnaires routinely do not say that the opinions of the seller are limited, a potential problem. Instead of just filling out a form, smart sellers take the route used by termite inspectors and complete forms by saying that they have checked "visible and accessible areas" of the home and within the bounds of their training, experience, and education regarding such matters have completed the survey.

A review of local listing forms will show an amazing variety of clauses and concepts. When looking at these documents, always remember three points.

First, contracts are negotiable, and listing agreements are contracts when signed. *There is no such thing as a "standard" listing agreement that you must accept*, if only because "everyone else" uses it. Make your own deal, the one that places your interests first.

Second, don't hesitate for a moment to have a listing form reviewed by an attorney—your attorney—before signing. Thousands of dollars are at stake, money that doesn't come easily to most of us.

Third, remember that a broker is your agent only *after* you sign a listing agreement. Until that form is signed, you're adversaries, each trying to get the best possible deal. You can bet a smart broker understands the value of a listing, and you should, too.

PICKING A BROKER

Given so many factors, so many issues, how do you choose one broker over another? There is no simple or easy answer because different sellers have different situations, needs, and perspectives. As a way to sort through the choices, however, here are important questions to ask when considering the use of a broker.

Is this person active in real estate?

Does he or she sell properties on a regular basis? If not, how do they network with other brokers, keep up with the latest sales, or know about the newest rules and regulations?

Is this person active in my neighborhood? It simply does no good to hire a broker whose "territory" includes 1,600 square miles.

Does the broker or agent have recent references, people you can contact directly? If not, why not?

Is the individual resourceful, enterprising, and entrepreneurial? Look at the materials they present, their ideas, and their approach to issues and problems.

Have you seen the broker or agent holding an open house?

If so, is this the type of person you want to represent you and your property?

Does the listing presentation offered by the broker or agent make sense? Has your home been reasonably priced? Can the price be justified by recent sales or currently available properties?

Do you have a personal, social, or business relationship with the individual? If so, will listing or not listing influence your non-real estate relationship? Does the individual understand that the selection of a broker is a business decision for you?

Is the broker part of the local MLS? If not, why not?

Is the broker part of a referral network? If so, how has this helped the broker in the past year?

What forms of promotion does the broker use? Classified ads? Television? Radio? Local newspapers? Direct mail? Networking with other brokers? Open houses?

Does the broker originate mortgages? If so, are you comfortable with the fact that the broker, your agent, may earn a fee by locating financing for the buyer?

Does the individual have a good knowledge of mortgage financing? If not, how can he or she help a buyer? How can this person develop a marketing plan?

Is the broker or agent rigid with regard to listing arrangements and marketing concepts? Can you negotiate a deal with this person that makes sense for you, or must you conform to the broker's usual standards and practices?

Do you instinctively feel you can trust this person?

Will the broker buy your home if it doesn't sell? So-called "guaranteed-sale" programs can be seductive, but they typically have several costs. One expense is that the commission on such deals is likely to be higher than an owner might otherwise pay.

A second item concerns pricing. A broker may offer to warrant the sale of a property, but at what price? Clearly it is not in the broker's best interest to offer the highest possible price, so buy-out prices equal to 82 to 88 percent of market value are likely. But then, who determines market value? The owner? An independent appraiser? The broker?

A third expense with guarantee programs can involve repairs. The broker may require owners to fix up and repair to make the property more salable. Such repairs can be seen as a cost of selling.

No deal is without costs and the real question raised by guaranteed sales is this: given the commission and sale price, is this the best you can do? For some owners, particularly those who need to move quickly or who are selling in a weak market, guaranteed sales can be attractive. The trick is to know the bottom line, to see how much you will have after all expenses have been deducted.

Does the broker offer resale warranties to make homes more attractive?

Considering the general level of nervousness that dogs many buyers, there is much to recommend a resale warranty, if only as something to create additional peace of mind.

A resale warranty is a guarantee of sorts backed by an insurance company. It says that if anything on a specified list of potential problems goes wrong, the expense for repairs and replacements is covered under the policy. There is usually a deductible amount with such policies, the variety of potential disasters is limited, and there are sometimes other fees as well.

In a market where homes need a marketing boost, resale warranties are cheap relative to a home sale. And to the extent that they make one property stand out, resale warranties have value.

Is the agent full-time or part-time?

Real estate brokers and agents are typically self-employed, independent contractors. They don't punch a time clock or work nine-to-five, so in a literal sense time on the job is not an issue.

By "full-time" what many brokers really mean are those who do nothing but work in real estate, as opposed to people who have a license but earn some or all of their income in other fields.

A Special Case

Sometimes it happens that you have a broker who has done everything promised and more, but still the house doesn't sell.

Should you dump the broker when the listing runs out?

If you have a broker who is working hard on your behalf, keeping promises, and acting professionally, then the broker is doing exactly what he or she was hired to do. It's a matter of personal preference, but the view here is that hardworking brokers are worth keeping. If the listing term has been reasonable for your community and price range, then extend it. That's a fair way to treat a broker who lives up to listing promises—and a good way to know that your property is being handled by a competent professional.

Time is simply not a measure of broker competence. An inept broker may work 80 hours a week, while a well-educated, proficient, skilled individual may produce more deals and more income laboring just 10 hours a week. Clearly you would prefer the "part-timer."

As real estate deals have become more complex, it has become increasingly difficult to be an effective part-time practitioner. The result is that while time on the job is not a solid measure of brokerage ability, time *is* needed to keep up with changing rules, new loan formats, community events that affect values, new technologies, and marketing techniques.

The true test of broker competence is performance. How well does the broker do his or her job? Is the broker out there marketing your home, protecting your interests, and getting the best possible deal for you? If so, that's someone you should consider.

The catch is that you can't know how a broker will perform until a listing has been signed. For this reason, it may make sense to have a listing with a kick-out clause that works like this: if you're not "satisfied" with the broker's performance, then the listing will end upon payment of the broker's costs to market your property, such as advertising, brochures, MLS fees, etc. There should be a protection period to assure that the broker is paid if someone introduced to the property during the listing period buys within 30 days (or whatever term) after the listing is ended. In addition, it should be agreed that the protection period will automatically terminate if the property is listed with another broker.

Competent brokers will have no trouble with a kick-out clause because they expect to perform. Alternatively, if a deal sours, smart brokers will want to move along to other properties where there is a better chance of success.

5
Hidden Issues

Look at any home sale and it will become quickly apparent that more than real estate is at stake.

Yes, a home is a storehouse of value, an asset that can be measured in dollars and cents. And when it comes time to sell, there's no doubt that every owner wants the best possible deal.

But for all the attention to money, there's more to a home—and more to homeselling—than cash.

The argument is not that cash is unimportant, or that a home should be sold for less than market value. Instead, the point is that to obtain the best possible sale results it pays to understand the hidden issues that are part of every real estate deal.

PSYCHOLOGY

For both buyers and sellers, a house holds important personal values. Where we live is an index of our status, financial success, and social standing. One broker who sells large homes gives each property a name: "The Crownwreath," "Belton Tower," or some such moniker; this is not because names make the homes larger or innately more valuable, but because formal names convey a sense of standing, importance, and prominence.

Sellers look at a home and they see where the family had barbecues, the doorway where children were measured as they grew, and the small stick planted long ago that is now a tree towering over the front yard. To the sellers, such markers have great personal value, but the marketplace is less sentimental.

While psychology is not to be ignored, it must be kept in focus. Sellers routinely price property at a given level because a particular number conveys a certain importance ("Well, I'm a wonderful person and therefore my home should sell for $300,000."). While ego is great, homes priced on the basis of owner self-perceptions are unlikely to sell quickly. And when such mispriced properties ultimately sell at a deflated value, you can bet the owner's ego will be deflated as well.

It thus becomes important to look at a home and recognize that the values you have are not shared by everyone. *Selling a home is a business transaction*, and you can be certain that pricing will be influenced more by comparable sales than by memories.

The attractive aspect about psychology, however, is that both buyers and sellers seek ego satisfaction. Buyers want status, evidence of what they have accomplished, and a standard by which they can be measured.

While you may not elect to name your home, psychological tools can help your sale. To the extent plausible, emphasize the ego factors that make your property stand out:

> *Association*: If you live in a community with executives, lawyers, doctors, and other professionals, be sure to say so. Professional buyers will see such a community as consistent with their image.

> *Cachet*: If your property is historic or unique, explain why it stands out.

> *Location*: Location is crucial and if your location is special—the highest point in town, the largest lot in Northville—make sure that buyers know.

> *Size*: Small may be beautiful, but big is generally preferred—especially when it comes to real estate. Rooms (and homes) that are elegant, graceful, and spacious carry with them certain values that many people covet.

> *Security*: A small home can always be marketed as a secure niche in the world, something practical buyers can own and afford even in turbulent times.

Psychological values stand out as a set of perceptions that can help or hurt your cause, depending on the extent to which they are a substitute for reality. So let the buyers fall in love with your home—but keep your eye on the bottom line.

CURRENT EVENTS

Picture a home on a quiet street and it may be hard to see the connection between real estate marketing and current events, but the tie-ins are there.

No one suggests that every news item—a dust storm in Peru, a revolt in Mongolia—directly influences the sale of your home. But to a greater extent than at any time in our history, home sales are less localized than in the past.

Imagine that Widget Industries, a vast multi-national corporation with factories in 15 countries, suddenly finds that it can manufacture (what else) widgets in the former People's Republic of Frombia at half the cost of that old plant in your town. Production moves overseas and 500 local people are tossed out of work. That means not only 500 fewer jobs, it also means reduced tax rolls, less money for local merchants, and—most important for our purposes—a smaller pool of potential buyers for your property.

In a similar fashion, if North Glumbus goes to war with South Glumbus, it may be that South Glumbians no longer buy U.S. Treasury bonds. Whether the cause of either side is just, unjust, or even comprehensible, investment funds to the United States are reduced. Given less foreign investment (supply) and ongoing demand, interest rates rise in the United States. Now, suddenly, the $100,000 mortgage that could be financed at 7 percent is only available at 7.5 percent, a difference of $33.91 a month. That may not seem like a lot, except that many buyers purchase homes on the cusp of affordability. If rates rise, even minutely, such purchasers either buy less or buy nothing, and—once again—your pool of potential buyers shrinks.

Not only can international events influence buyers, they can also sway your situation. Suppose you have a one-year adjustable-rate mortgage (ARM). The new rate is based on the interest level as of a given date and, as it happens, hostilities throughout Glumbia break out two weeks before your rate changes. Suddenly rates edge up and as a result your interest cost for the coming year is 1 percent higher than you expected.

International events, decisions in Washington, or matters 6,000 miles from your neighborhood now play a role in the local homeselling process. The problem for a seller is that your property is unchanged, but somehow its value rises or falls because of circumstances you cannot control.

We are each hostages to developments beyond our reach, situations we cannot possibly change or influence. It means that while we, as home-sellers, would prefer a placid marketplace, current events make the marketing process less predictable and more risky than in the past. That's not good news, but it's the way the world works.

TIME

Ecclesiastes tells us there is a "time for every purpose," a concept that certainly applies to real estate.

The best time to sell your home is likely to be based on local patterns rather than national trends. Vacation property is best sold before or during the "season"; the market for urban and suburban property is usually best during the spring and summer (because parents want to get their children into new schools at the start of the academic year); and demand for midwestern farmland peaks after harvest but before leasing, say from December to early March.

Time is also important in another sense. The process of selling a home, even in the best circumstances, is likely to take several months.

- Before you can offer a property for sale it must be cleaned, repaired, and prepped for public viewing.
- Once on the market, a home may remain available for weeks, months, and sometimes years. How long a home remains on the market will be influenced by general economic conditions, local events (a new mall opening down the road, a factory closing), the time of year, how your property compares to others, pricing, condition, etc.
- After a sales contract is ratified, it typically takes six to eight weeks before the deal can be closed, time needed to obtain financing, check the title, and prepare paperwork.

To assure that matters are further complicated, selling times also relate to home prices. Entry-level homes are likely to sell with greater rapidity than $5 million estates, the theory being that there are more entry-level buyers than members of the rich and famous.

NO COMPARISONS

Like Windsor Castle or Jefferson's Monticello, your home has the distinction of being the only one in the world. It is unique; no other house is exactly or precisely like yours, even if you live in a subdivision with 10,000 similar houses.

How can this be?

A central tenet of real estate is that all homes are distinctive, that each offers "nonhomogeneity."

One reason homes are different concerns physics. Only one home can occupy a given site. But not only are locations unique, so too is each deal.

The selling price of a property is determined at one point in time under specific conditions through the agreement of a buyer and seller. At any other point in time, with any other conditions, or with different buyers and sellers, the price and terms for a given property may be different.

The unique nature of real estate—and real estate sales—is important.

- It means that one broker cannot sell a house "faster" than another broker in the open market. If broker Smith sold a home in one week there is absolutely no assurance that your home will sell as quickly if you list with Smith, or at all.
- Since all homes and all deals are different, there is no *precise* basis for comparison.
- While the sale price of one house may be a general index of value, it's not an absolute assurance that another house will sell for a specific price.
- A "good" sale today may be a bad deal tomorrow because conditions can change.
- One broker cannot "guarantee" to sell a home for more money or better terms than another broker in the open market because there is no basis for comparison. Like fingerprints, individual home sales are simply different.
- Average results, such as the amount of time it takes to sell a typical house in your community, may not relate to your specific property.

NET BENEFIT

Figuring out why someone wants to sell a home, at least in a financial sense, may seem fairly obvious: top money and the best possible terms.

But problems arise when sellers translate "top money and the best possible terms" into the "highest sale price."

Sale prices, in and of themselves, may not define a deal. To see why, consider that the Conklin property sold for $150,000 while the Rivera home was bought for $145,000. Since $150,000 is bigger than $145,000, it looks as though Conklin will have the bigger bank account once closing is completed. Or will she?

Conklin sold her home for $150,000 and promised the buyers that she would pay the first $1,000 in closing costs, fix the roof ($3,500), and pay two points ($2,400 in this case). At closing, Conklin also paid a $9,000 sales commission to her broker. Add the figures and a deal that looks like a $150,000 sale produces a net benefit to the seller of just $134,100 ($150,000 less $15,900).

Rivera, in contrast, sold her property by herself for $145,000. She made no concessions, paid $400 for advertising and $350 for legal fees, and walked away from closing with $144,250.

These examples are simplified for our purposes, but the basic principle stands out: *the financial success of a home sale is measured in terms of its net benefit, the amount you get at closing.*

The best time to remember the net benefit is that shining instant when someone says, "Gee, we love your house and we'll pay your price." So far, so good, but without a careful review of the fine print "your price" may not be good enough.

PRICING REPORTS

A staple in every real estate market are reports by local newspapers, magazines, governments, and brokerage organizations measuring community sales and prices. In almost every instance you can be certain that such reports are both statistically correct and more or less irrelevant.

Pricing reports may show average sale figures (the total dollar volume of sales in a given area divided by the number of transactions) or median statistics (the price at which half the homes cost more and half cost less). Both measures are invariably tainted.

One problem is that sale reports are commonly too broad. A report that lists sale prices by ZIP code, for example, may cover several square miles in a suburban community. But your neighborhood, say 500 homes in the Westmont subdivision, may be bigger, or smaller, than typical homes in your ZIP code. You may have better schools, more desirable access to downtown, or, unfortunately, a large number of crack houses. The result is that price reports for a ZIP code, county, city, state, or congressional district may not relate to your neighborhood.

What is being sold also influences price reports. Imagine that last year 100 single-family homes at $150,000 each were sold in your ZIP code and, as well, 125 townhouses marketed at an average price of $75,000. In this situation we have 225 sales, a total volume of $24,375,000, an average price of $108,333, and a median price of $141,667.

Now, suppose this year we sell 150 townhouses at $75,000 apiece and 75 detached homes at $150,000 each. We have 225 sales, gross revenues of $22,500,000, sale prices that average $100,000, and median prices set at $125,000.

Comparing the two years, the number of sales remains unchanged, but average sale prices have declined 8.3 percent while median values have fallen by almost 12 percent.

You could also look at these figures another way: neither the price of single-family homes nor the value of townhouses changed at all. Values held steady over a two-year period. What changed was the composition of home sales, a movement toward lower-priced townhouses in this example.

Unfortunately, all-inclusive sale prices remain a quick and sloppy way to evaluate market trends. In theory there is nothing wrong with such valuations, but in practice such generalized studies may not parallel events in your neighborhood.

As a seller it is crucially important to consider local sales trends when pricing your home, rather than overall market activity. How local? As local as appropriate, which may mean a given building, a small neighborhood, all "Heathrow" models in your subdivision, or whatever.

Alternatively, learn to play the pricing game. If values are generally up, it's not your job to demand a rigorous accounting of the overall marketplace. If values are generally down, you must define your marketplace in a positive manner ("Sure, prices are down around town, but you know, Hemlock Valley is a very special area. We don't have a lot of high-priced homes with six bedrooms that sit on the market for months at a time. Instead, we have homes for entry-level buyers, so our situation here has been positive during the past year and we've had a lot of activity.").

LEVERAGE

If you were last active in the real estate marketplace five or 10 years ago, no doubt you see changes all around. Uniform marketing concepts, contracts, and costs have given way to consumer-driven diversity. There are now traditional brokers, discounters, and flat-fee firms to serve your needs. And, of course, there is also the option of self-selling.

As someone with a clear sense of self-interest, it's your job to seek advantage wherever you can within the limits of law and morality. This means you want people to compete for your business (selling your property, doing your legal work, whatever). The test in such competitions is your sense of who can do the best job for you, however you alone define "best."

In some cases it may be difficult to act for our own betterment. As social creatures we want to avoid conflict; we want to be "nice," to appease rather than confront. But selling a home is an adversarial process. The buyer wants to pay you less and professionals want you to pay more. If you accede to everyone's demands and interests, you will be left with less than you deserve.

It is because you can make choices that you have power. If you let other people make choices for you, if you are unduly dependent on other people, if you do not establish what you want and how it is to be done, then your leverage declines. You should welcome advice from lawyers, brokers, lenders, buyers, family members, co-workers, and friends; use what you can, but leave no doubt that you alone are the final and absolute decision-maker.

And as the ultimate arbitrator, remember whose interests are at stake and whose interests come first.

DISCRIMINATION

Discrimination represents one of the most difficult issues of our time, a matter found again and again in the real estate marketing process.

Since the Civil Rights Act of 1866 it has been flat-out illegal to discriminate on the basis of race, yet when testers in this day and age look at housing the results are as predictable as the morning's sunrise: a strong whiff of discrimination haunts real estate sales, rentals, and financing.

Today it is illegal to discriminate on the base of race, religion, gender, disability, familial status, or national origin. In many areas, it is also illegal to discriminate for other reasons, such as sexual preference or the presence of children. If you discriminate, or if your agent or subagent discriminates, the penalties, legal bills, and approbation can be enormous.

Since laws and moral conviction have not resolved the issue of real estate discrimination, perhaps it's worth considering self-interest. Simply put, sellers (and brokers) who discriminate reduce the pool of potential buyers for the properties they market. And as the pool shrinks, there is less demand, less competition, and ultimately less need to pay a premium price for a given property.

In a logical universe, sellers and brokers should do whatever they can to get as many people as humanly possible interested in the homes they want to sell. Whether those humans are one color or another, married, unmarried, straight, gay, disabled, or born somewhere else is irrelevant. What counts is whether a given party is ready, willing, and able to buy at a price and terms acceptable to a seller. If so, there's a deal to be made.

6
Preparing Your Home

When home sales are hot, just about any property, in just about any condition, is magically salable. Unfortunately, when markets moderate, slow down, stop, or fall, a new circumstance emerges: the need to get a home in "show" condition.

To understand the value of show condition, imagine going to a house where the owners have not bothered to fix up, clean up, or repair. The house may be perfectly livable and relatively neat, but if the faucet leaks, maybe other things have not been fixed. Maybe big, costly things that you can't see are broken, rotting, or in need of repair.

What really happens with a home not prepared for sale is that an illusion is broken; the buyer's belief that a home is in great condition is undermined and with it the necessity to pay top dollar or make an immediate offer. After all, odds are the home will still be available a month from now, because who wants to buy a questionable property? And in a month, maybe the price will be more reasonable.

Fixing up also has important values when listing a home for sale. A logical broker will look at your property as a business deal, a commodity to sell for the greatest possible return. The more attractive your home, the more likely it is to sell, the greater the broker's interest.

At the same time, since a home in show condition is an attractive commodity, you—the seller—gain leverage when dealing with a broker, leverage that might be converted into a lower fee or better terms.

Fixing up thus emerges as a central obligation. Sellers want a good price and a quick sale, but such goals are clouded when a home is not properly prepared.

Preparing a home for sale begins with a careful analysis of what is usual and customary in your community. Visit nearby open houses and model homes on a Sunday afternoon, look around, make notes, and ask these questions:

- What has been done? Have the owners fixed up, repaired, replaced, or painted? If so, what items have been improved prior to sale?
- What has not been done? What have the owners failed to do that would make their property more salable? What are the small items that have been left undone? The big ones? The items that make an impression?
- As you approach the property, is there anything—good or bad—that catches your eye? As an example, has the front door been painted?
- Has the outside of the home been well tended? That is, has the grass been mowed, shrubs trimmed, trees pruned?
- Have the owners or their agents cleaned up common areas such as sidewalks and streets?
- Do the owners or their agents have maintenance records, warranty information, or instruction manuals?
- Have the owners kept paint-can labels so that colors can be matched?

After a careful survey of available properties—properties with which your home may be competing in the not-too-distant future—it is then possible to begin the preparation process.

THE FIX-UP RULE

In preparing a home for sale, sellers should be guided by the old real estate saying that buyers tend to seek the least expensive home in the most expensive neighborhood they can afford.

Suppose there is a neighborhood with three-bedroom $100,000 homes, but one family—we'll call them the Browns—has added on and fixed up to the point where their property now has five bedrooms, a pool, and a $200,000 price tag.

How salable is this house? On an objective basis—square footage, the cost of expansions, the expense of putting in the pool—this home may well be worth $200,000, but only if it can be moved. People who want a $200,000 home will buy in a neighborhood where most of the houses cost

$200,000. In fact, if at all possible, most buyers would greatly prefer to pay $200,000 in neighborhoods where homes are priced at $250,000; $300,000; or even more.

The fixing-up rule provides an important benchmark that sellers should not ignore: prepare your home before placing it on the market, but don't over-improve.

Here are tests to consider before investing in repairs and refurbishing.

Is the improvement necessary?

Imagine that you have a dishwasher that works. Not great, but it runs. Maybe it will last another year or two before it conks out completely.

The dishwasher is clearly not a gem, but then to whom are you selling? In an entry-level home a dishwasher—any dishwasher—may be better than anything the buyers have ever had. To them, your dishwasher may be the most wonderful appliance in the house. In a mid-priced or upper-bracket property, it can be assumed that would-be buyers have dishwashers, know what to expect, and expect more than you are offering.

In the case of the entry-level house the preferred course will be to leave the dishwasher as is, say nothing, and see what happens. If someone wants to buy the house but demands a new dishwasher as part of the deal, that may be acceptable. Alternatively, if the buyer says nothing, you're ahead $500.

For mid-priced and upper-bracket homes the story is different. More money and greater expectations are involved. An owner will want to replace the old dishwasher with a new model, or offer a credit to buyers at closing so that the purchasers can pick the brand and model of their choosing

Does the improvement make the property more attractive?

Adding improvements can be a tricky matter for several reasons.

First, the wrong improvement can actually reduce the salability of a home. A pool, for instance, may be great for some people but not for others. Those "others" will not buy the property because they will not want the hassles, upkeep, and liability associated with a pool.

Second, a big improvement must be consistent with the neighborhood. If you have a $20,000 addition to the property, it's only natural to want a $20,000 return—or more if you can get it. The catch is that a $20,000 improvement may mean that you are trying to sell a home for $170,000 in a neighborhood where properties consistently cost $150,000. That's not the way to price housing, or to obtain a quick sale

Who are you trying to satisfy?

The purpose of fixing up and repairing should be seen within the strict boundaries of one issue: will the home be more salable? If the purpose of an improvement is to enhance your ego satisfaction or one-up the neighbors, the probability is that dollars are being wasted.

Will you get your money out?

Surveys are published yearly by several magazines that purport to show the financial benefits associated with given improvements. Such surveys, to be polite, should be regarded with skepticism.

One issue with improvement returns is that preferences vary around the country. An outdoor pool in Massachusetts has less utility than one built in Georgia.

Precise location is also a factor. A pool built down the street from an attractive community facility will have a different value than a pool that is the only one in the neighborhood.

But the biggest problem with home-improvement surveys is that they attempt to measure the immeasurable. A home with a $20,000 addition does not automatically increase the property's value by 20 grand. Maybe the house will only command $15,000 more than like properties, or in a down market maybe nothing.

The point is that owners should fix up before selling, but grandiose additions should be seen for what they are: expenditures that may not make the house more valuable or more salable

WHAT TO THROW OUT

Given the pros and cons above, sellers should prepare homes with three thoughts in mind.

1) Always remember the buyer's maxim: buyers tend to purchase the least expensive home in the most expensive neighborhood they can afford.

2) Never over-improve. Be consistent with the neighborhood; otherwise you are likely to lose money.

3) When plausible, view improvements as a bargaining tool so that dollars are not needlessly committed up front. For example, instead of spending $3,000 to replace carpets that may be acceptable to most buyers, do nothing. If it becomes necessary to haggle, offer a $1,000 carpet allowance. If that doesn't work, try $2,000. Explain that with an allowance the buyers can choose their own colors and materials.

Considering these guidelines as well as your tour of open houses and model homes, here is a checklist for homeowners.

Clutter. When you sell your home, movers will seek your business, at which time you will discover that some charge by the quantity of items to be relocated. Being rational at that moment—and seen in the light of transportation costs—the decision will then be made to dump a variety of once-cherished possessions.

As a seller the best advice is: don't wait. Do it now, before you sell. Cleaning out your home will not only cut moving expenses, it will also make your property more salable because it will seem more spacious.

One absolutely classic case involved a gentleman who, for one reason or another, wanted to sell a residential apartment that had somehow been transformed into a warehouse of sorts. He didn't actually live there—he couldn't, because each room was filled from floor to ceiling with a massive number of brown cartons. While each room was visible from a hallway (which was also lined with cartons), there was no way to actually see the size of the apartment or for a buyer to envision how his or her possessions might be laid out.

Many homes, as well, are filled with clutter, and clutter reduces salability. Basements, closets, cabinets, garages, and storage sheds are routinely filled with possessions that might be used at a later date, but usually aren't.

Here are several steps to take:

Children. If you have adult children, make a list of specific items that they can use and ask if they would like them.

Garage/House Sales. Turn miscellaneous stuff into money with a garage sale. A suburban staple, garage sales are a good way to empty a house and determine at the same time which items should be given away.

Better Furnishings. If not a garage sale, sell through a consignment shop. The usual deal is that the shop gets a fee for the sale and you get access to a retail location. No guarantees, but not a bad deal.

Old Appliances. Clean, working appliances can often be donated to charitable groups. Call around to locate groups that will pick up directly from your property.

Old Clothes. Clean, warm clothing in good repair—no matter how old—can be donated to charitable groups.

Old Bedding. Clean sheets and blankets can be donated to charitable groups, but mattresses can be a problem. Local health regulations may limit the ability of charitable groups to accept used mattresses, a major problem because daily trash collectors are also unlikely to take such objects. In the worst case, earmark mattresses for the dump.

Old Furniture. Some charities will accept used furniture, others will not. Look for charities that pick up at your door.

Trash Collectors. Street-side pick-ups commonly exclude construction materials, furniture, mattresses, and appliances. Although not a choice for everyone, some homeowners have been known to break up materials so that over a period of weeks entire patio sets and other items gradually go into municipal trucks.

Special Pick-Up. Some communities provide special pick-up service. You call the trash collectors and arrange for a truck to come by and pick up large or unusual items. This service may be free once or twice a year, or available at a nominal cost.

Dumps. Dump rules vary around the country. You may face a dump fee, particularly if your "deposit" exceeds a certain weight. In other places, community dump sites consist of no more than a line of large dumpsters available to everyone without cost.

REPAIRS VERSUS IMPROVEMENTS

Once a home is cleaned out, the next step is to determine what repairs and improvements are required. The choices will vary from property to property, but one baseline point should be established.

An "improvement" should be seen as a big-ticket item that will provide value and enjoyment over many years. A repair is something such as painting or pruning that is cosmetic and minimal.

The government says that "improvements" can be deducted from the sale price when you sell your home to determine your profit and loss. For example, suppose you bought your home for $125,000 ten years ago, added a $12,000 garage, and sold the property for $175,000. In this situation your "basis" is $137,000 (the purchase price plus the $12,000 improvement) and your profit is $38,000 ($175,000 less $137,000).

A repair or fix-up may be deductible, as well. The general rule is that repairs made 90 days prior to a sale and paid for within 30 days of closing can be written off. If you paid $185,000 for your home, spent $5,000 painting prior to sale, and sold the property for $300,000, then you have a profit of $110,000.

Given the government's tax policies, it makes sense to keep records showing when capital improvements were made and how much they cost. A string of canceled checks is also valuable.

It also makes sense to make repairs within the bargaining process, rather than before. If you spend $2,000 painting but the house doesn't sell for six months, that money is not deductible. If you sell the property and as a condition of the sale agree to repaint, then your cost is likely to be within 90 days of the sale and therefore deductible.

For the latest rules, speak with a certified public accountant (CPA), tax attorney, or enrolled agent for more information. Also review IRS form 2119 and publication 523.

FORTY STEPS TOWARD A BETTER IMAGE

By now the general outlines of what needs to be done for your particular house should be taking shape. You want the house in show condition. You want to spend as little as possible. Here are 40 low-cost steps to consider before placing your property on the market.

1) Remove clutter.

2) Paint. If you can't paint everything, or don't need to, paint those areas most visible, such as the front door and doorway.

3) If wooden doors and windows stick, plane them down.

4) Wash all windows.

5) Rake and mow lawns. Make certain that drainage is away from the house.

6) Trim dead trees and bushes. Convert dead limbs into firewood.

7) Clean carpets with a carpet machine.

8) Clean and caulk sinks, basins, and bathtubs.

9) Clean under sinks. If a drain pipe leaks, replace it and repair any water damage.

10) Replace dead light bulbs.

11) Clean out gutters and downspouts.

12) If musty, air out basement areas.

13) Purchase an outlet tester from Radio Shack and check all outlets to assure they are properly connected. Have an electrician repair as appropriate.

14) Replace old furnace filters with new ones.

15) Remove grease and oil from garage floors.

16) For brick homes 40 years of age and older: check for missing mortar and cracks. Repoint and replace as required.

17) Plant flowers appropriate for the season.

18) If required, rent storage space for several months to keep excess goods.

19) Clean appliances. This means, within the bounds of safety and common sense, more than a usual cleaning. For instance, a toothbrush is ideal for cleaning out small grooves in rubber gaskets on refrigerators and dishwashers. Be aware that many cleaning compounds are powerful chemicals and be certain to follow all instructions. Excellent ventilation is particularly important.

20) Test all appliances and equipment. Anything that does not work should be fixed, replaced, or removed.

21) Gather all appliance and equipment manuals in one place.

22) Keep paint-can labels so colors can be matched.

23) Make basement areas bright by painting cinderblock walls white.

24) Consider painting concrete floors gray. Look for paints that limit slippage.

25) Get rid of old chemicals such as ancient paint cans, garden supplies, used oil, etc. Speak with community trash administrators for advice regarding proper disposal.

26) Have a professional chimney sweep clear fireplaces and chimneys to remove soot, ash, and creosote.

27) If you have a shop, put away sharp tools and turn off the electric supply for equipment such as lathes, drill presses, etc.

28) If you have a home office, place valued papers in locked storage. One approach is to take a regular closet handle and replace it with a lockable device.

29) Clean curtains and drapes.

30) Patch, seal, and refinish driveways as required.

31) Repair concrete walks and steps.

32) Insulate as appropriate for your area.

33) Examine bathroom areas with care. Check toilets for running and leakage. Running toilets can lose thousands of gallons of water per year. Fix seals and valves, as required. Replace old toilet seats. Remove mildew from baths and showers. Most mildew on tile can be removed with soap, water, and a good brush. Be extremely careful when using chemical agents, follow directions, and be certain to have adequate ventilation. Dispose of chemical agents with care.

34) Clean out basement floor drains, and outside drains, as necessary.

35) Be certain that you have smoke detectors and that they are in working condition. For battery-powered models, replace batteries. Note that many communities now require working smoke detectors as a sale condition.

36) Grease garage-door slides.

37) Check the intercom and burglar alarm.

38) Vacuum vents, grates, and radiators, as appropriate.

39) Replace all cracked glass. Note that special safety glass is likely to be required for storm-door inserts.

40) Remove old food cans to create the sense of more kitchen space. Where possible, contribute to a local food bank.

Most of the items above can be done at little or no cost by owners. But while it may be cheap, fixing up can take weeks of ongoing effort at night and on weekends. This is not a casual process to be done a week before you want to sell. Plan ahead, and use the list above as a starting point. It will mean money in your pocket down the road.

7
So What's It Worth?

At the heart of every home sale is the issue of price, one sure measure of value that everyone can understand.

More art than science, offering prices represent a starting point in the bargaining process, a target value that must be selected with care. Set the price too high and buyers will shun your property. Set the price too low and you'll get less than the value you deserve.

To make the pricing dance even more complex, every seller goes into the marketplace at a disadvantage. Why? Because good bargaining means letting the other guy (or gal) mention a price first.

Think about it this way. You go to buy a used car. The owner says "I'll take $4,500 for it, as is." Like magic, there is now a ceiling on the deal. You can buy the car or not buy the car, but you will not pay more than $4,500 and there is a good chance you will pay less.

But suppose the car owner takes a different approach. Instead of mentioning a specific price, imagine if the owner says, "I've had this car for a few years now and it has really given me good service. What do you think it's worth?"

If you mention a price it may or may not be a ceiling, but it certainly will be a floor. You might say, "Well, I'll offer $4,000 for it," and the owner can tell you that he was expecting "more."

"More" is one of those great expressions that lacks precise meaning. More than what? The answer is uncertain, but one matter is clear: by first bringing up a specific price, part of the deal has already been determined.

In a similar fashion, an offering price generally defines the top value you will receive. Place your home on the market for $195,000 and there is little reason for buyers to offer $196,000. Sure, there have been instances where sellers receive premium amounts that top asking prices, but such bidding wars are rare, especially when markets are not superheated.

The negotiation process punishes those who speak first, yet somebody has to set the haggling and dickering in motion. In residential real estate, that "someone" is typically the homeseller, the person who makes the first move and thereby establishes the top price.

Whether the asking price will also be the final sale price is not certain, but since the offering price establishes the top of the market, it follows that sellers benefit when offering prices and selling prices are as close together as possible. Seen another way, since you are setting the highest possible value for your property, it pays (literally) not to start too low.

Figuring the value of your home can be as easy as reading the Sunday classified ads or so complex as to require the services of an Oxford don. No matter, it has to be done and here's how to start.

THREE APPRAISAL METHODS

In some cases it's fairly simple to calculate a sales price. If you live in a subdivision and 22 Croftmont models like yours have sold in the past three months for prices ranging from $152,000 to $153,000, you can bet that a lengthy market evaluation is unnecessary. You can price your home somewhat higher, but the end result is going to be within or near the established price range.

Less clear is the situation in a neighborhood that has evolved over the past 75 years and where every house is different. The value of a single house in such neighborhoods can be a matter of considerable contention because the usual clues—such items as past sales and similar properties—may have debatable relevance, if they exist at all.

To figure the value of your property, follow the practices used by real estate appraisers and brokers.

One approach is to consider how much it would cost to replace your home. The replacement-value system works nicely if the property in question is a church or synagogue, and in theory it can work as well for homes. In reality, replacement-value appraisals are best used for properties where there are few, if any, structures of comparable size, design, or purpose—not the situation faced by most homesellers.

Another way to look at home values is to say, aha, this place can generate money if it is rented, say $15,000 a year. Deduct operating expenses worth $3,500 annually and $11,500 remains. If an investor seeks a "capitalization rate" of 10 percent, then an offer of $115,000 might be forth-coming ($11,500 times 1 divided by .10). If the cap rate is 7 percent, then the property is worth $164,285.

The income approach works fine for buildings, shopping malls, and vast industrial parks, so if your home can be used for commercial purposes, if it can be converted into an apartment complex or service-station site, then the income approach can be a useful measure of value.

Most homes, of course, have only one use and that is residential. The usual, traditional, and customary way to value residential property is to take a close look at past sales and current offerings in your community.

To develop comparisons, you need to look at homes that have sold in your neighborhood for the past six to 12 months, and you need as well to look at the homes now on the market.

Looking at currently available properties means setting aside a few Sunday afternoons to visit open houses. This is not a casual outing, how-ever; your goal is to find specific information. For each property, list the following items, as appropriate.

1) Address.

2) Name of broker or owner.

3) Phone number.

4) Date visited.

5) Asking price.

6) Number of bedrooms.

7) Number of full baths (at least a sink, toilet, and shower).

8) Number of half-baths (at least a sink and toilet).

9) Condition of baths: move-in; clean; or in need of repairs, updating, wallpaper, or caulking.

10) Type of kitchen. In general terms, a small kitchen is a "galley" kitchen, better yet is an "eat-in" kitchen, and better still is a "country" kitchen, which is merely a big version of an eat-in kitchen.

11) Appliances. Look for appliances that are new (installed Tuesday), modern (offering today's gizmos and gadgets), well maintained (clean), and functional (working).

12) Carpets. Are they clean, attractive, worn?

13) Closets. Are they large? Small? Fitted with built-in storage?

14) Floors. Are they clean? Worn? Not visible (because of carpeting)?

15) Paint. Is the property painted? In need of paint? Painted in hideous colors?

16) Basement. Is it dry? Clean? Usable?

17) Attic. Is it dry? Clean? Usable?

18) HVAC. Do the heating, ventilation, and air-conditioning systems work? Is there an electronic air filter? A dehumidifier in working order?

19) Is there a garage? Carport? On-site parking? Is there an automatic garage-door opener in working condition? Is the driveway in good repair? Is there off-street parking?

20) Is there a working intercom? Burglar alarm?

21) Is the exterior well tended? Are lawns cut, hedges trimmed, trees pruned, etc.?

22) Does the property have special features such as an in-ground pool, toolshed, play set, fencing?

23) In general terms, would you rate the house as excellent, average, or needs work?

24) Size. Is the home bigger or smaller than yours? The lot?

25) Does the home have solid curb appeal, a look that is impressive and attractive?

At first the list above may seem a little complex, but after a while it will help you understand values. You will soon be able to see that an extra bedroom is worth $5,000, while an old kitchen knocks $3,000 off the sales price. You'll be able to see what features are attractive and appropriate in your community, and which are costly duds.

FINDING PAST AND CURRENT SALES

To value homes, you need to look at properties now on the market (potential competitors), and you need as well to look at recent past sales.

One way to obtain past sale information is to call the public records office in your community and ask where you can look up past sales. Home-sale information is public in most jurisdictions, but not all.

Another approach is to clip sale information that appears from time to time in local newspapers. In major metropolitan areas, however, published sale reports should be viewed as incomplete because many sales are not listed.

If you're selling a co-op, then it is possible that no public records exist to track sales in your building or project. The reason is that co-op sales represent the transfer of stock rather than real estate, so recordation in the usual sense is not required. In the case of a co-op sale, speak with co-op officers to obtain past sale information since each sale must be approved by the co-op board.

For condos, speak with your association officers for sale information. They will generally be familiar with recent transactions and the association may even keep files to track activity and sales.

Perhaps the cheapest and easiest way to get comparable information is from the agents you meet at open houses, people you may wish to one day employ.

As you visit each property, consider how the agent acts. Is the agent helpful and articulate? Truthful? Knowledgeable about the house and the community? The type of person you would want to represent your interests?

Once you have met one or more agents, it's always possible to call and ask for help in pricing your home, a request with several implications.

If you make an appointment with a doctor or attorney and ask for advice, you can bet that a bill will soon be in the mail for the use of professional time. With real estate the situation is different, much to the benefit of homeowners.

Brokers and agents make their money when others buy and sell property. If you're a broker, you want to help a prospective homeseller because by being helpful you may get a listing, the right to sell the property.

In theory, a broker should charge for providing sales data and other marketing information, but in practice it doesn't happen. The reason is that more than two million people have real estate licenses and if broker Smith wants to charge for pricing information, then to get a competitive edge broker Jones will offer the same information without cost.

In approaching agents, however, it is important to play the game fairly. Don't tell Smith and Jones that you will list with one or the other if your true intention is to act as a self-seller. Don't promise anything. Instead, explain the situation as it is:

"We're thinking of selling our property in the next few months. We have not listed our home with anyone, and it is entirely possible that we may act as self-sellers. At this stage we have not made a firm decision. We want to get more information about pricing and marketing in our neighborhood. If you would like to meet with us and discuss the pricing and marketing of our home, we can get together with you on Wednesday evening at 7:30."

The broker at this point can make an appointment or not, as he or she prefers. But if you were a broker, what would you do? Your business is based on your ability to list and sell houses. Meeting new people in a businesslike manner is an opportunity to show off your skills and abilities.

No less important, an informed broker knows the facts. According to a

1991 study by the National Association of Realtors, most sellers (69 percent) will use a broker. Some will try to sell by themselves but will ultimately use an agent (8 percent). A few sellers will work differently, first using an agent and then selling directly (4 percent).

Recognizing that most sellers hire a professional, a smart broker makes the appointment. He or she knows that valuable professional time is at risk, but it's a cost of doing business.

Not only will a smart broker make an appointment, the broker will go further. The odds are that most sellers will hire a broker, so the real competition is to determine which broker will be hired. To make the best possible impression, a good broker will do more than write down a few numbers on the back of an envelope. Instead, you are likely to receive a computer-generated kit showing past sales, current listings, a baseline marketing plan, and background information about the broker. In effect, a complete marketing study.

As a seller—whether you want to hire a broker or not—you should be willing to meet with brokers active in your neighborhood. It can be educational and worthwhile to hear different opinions, to see how different brokers present themselves, and to hear how each might market your property.

It is also wise to carefully consider what is being said. If you meet with three or four brokers and one prices your property substantially higher or lower than the others, you need to ask why. Is the broker simply bidding high to get the listing? Bidding low to produce a quick sale? Or, is a significantly different value justified, even if it is a minority opinion?

Throughout the listening process, go back to the idea that buyers tend to purchase the least expensive home in the most expensive neighborhood they can afford. Be leery of brokers who suggest offering prices well in excess of neighborhood norms, and watch out as well for brokers who would sell your home cheap and pocket a quick commission for their trouble.

APPRAISERS

Brokers provide pricing and marketing information without cost because their profit is elsewhere in the deal. In effect, marketing information is a loss leader, one influenced by the broker's perception of your property as a business deal.

In addition to brokers, you can pay an appraiser to value your home, a choice that may be worthwhile in certain circumstances.

An appraiser is an independent party paid to render an "estimate" of reasonable value. The appraiser is paid for rendering a service, not for picking a particular number that you like or that will result in additional business. The result is a system where an appraisal should be seen as an independent, informed judgment by a competent professional.

That said, the appraisal process runs from neutral to hostile where the interests of sellers are concerned.

The point is not that appraisers are biased but rather that they tend to be conservative, a conservatism born from practical considerations.

In the usual case, a residential appraiser is not hired by an owner. Instead, an appraiser is called into a situation only after a deal has been struck and a price established.

Not only is an appraiser not hired by a seller, he or she is also not hired by a purchaser.

If not the buyer or seller, then who hires an appraiser?

The answer, in most cases, is the lender, and the lender's interests are separate and apart from either buyer or seller.

The lender wants to make certain that if the buyer screws up and defaults on the mortgage, the property has sufficient worth so that it can be sold for enough money to pay off the loan.

An appraiser's job can be seen as nothing more than protecting lender interests. An appraiser wants to assure that a property exists and that it has sufficient value to justify the lender's investment. This orientation means that appraisers tend to be conservative because they have no incentive to inflate prices.

Having explained why appraisers tend to be conservative, do you want your home appraised before it is placed on the market?

If you are dissatisfied with your ability to check comparable properties and you are not pleased with the pricing answers provided by local brokers, then an appraisal can make sense. An appraisal can also make sense to affirm the information given to you by local brokers and agents, should you feel such affirmation is necessary.

Appraisals can also be used as marketing tools. If your home is appraised at $155,000, then you can advertise that fact.

Additionally, if you obtain a VA or FHA appraisal, you can then advertise that your property is "VA appraised at $110,000" or "FHA appraised at $74,200." Such appraisals tell buyers (and brokers) that your home can be financed with VA or FHA mortgages and that a given worth has been officially validated.

Appraisers are now licensed and many belong to professional associations that provide instruction and certification. To order a conventional appraisal, check in the phone book under "real estate appraisers." For FHA and VA appraisals, contact local FHA and VA offices for lists of approved appraisers in your community. When speaking with FHA and VA officials, ask if the appraisal from one agency can be used for the other. Also, ask how long the appraisal will remain valid.

Are there any negatives to getting an appraisal up front? Four stand out.

First, an independent appraisal costs money whether or not you sell the house.

Second, appraisals have a limited shelf life, say 90 days to six months, depending on the lender and the loan program. If an appraisal is too old, the buyer will have to get a new one.

Third, you may not like the appraisal. If you think your home should sell for $135,000 and the appraiser says $129,000, you've paid for an appraisal you may not want to use.

Fourth, if you think having an appraisal will speed the financing process for your buyer, you may be right. Some lenders will accept appraisals ordered by sellers, but usually within narrow conditions. For instance, the appraiser must be on the lender's list of approved appraisers, the appraisal report must be timely, and it will only be accepted subject to the lender's review.

If you decide to go the up-front appraisal route, help your cause by having the home in "show" condition when the appraiser arrives. Don't tell the appraiser about all the glorious repairs you're going to make, have them in place so the appraiser can use them to generate a higher and better value.

DO ASSESSMENTS COUNT?

Whenever home values are discussed it is inevitable that the subject of tax assessments will arise.

Assessments establish property values for the purpose of calculating taxes at the state and local level. Political reality, however, dictates that assessment practices vary and that many issues not related to property values are well within the assessment process.

In urban areas, for example, governments strive to keep assessments low to prevent gentrification by taxation. In other words, if assessments rise quickly, so do tax assessments, and when tax assessments go up those on fixed incomes such as the elderly and the poor may not be able to keep their homes. This is particularly galling in those instances where someone bought a home 40 years ago, paid off the mortgage, and now lives on a small pension.

To have balance in the system (and to keep politicians employed), jurisdictions routinely give credits to older citizens and those with limited incomes. There are often different rates for residential properties and rental properties, even when both are identical. The property tax for a home is routinely based on the purchase price, which means that two identical homes can have different assessment values depending on which one was bought most recently. Many governments evaluate houses once every three or four years, not current enough when markets rise or fall. And to confuse matters further, there are limitations in many jurisdictions that place a ceiling on property-tax increases.

All of which means that an assessment may not be related to current market values. The probability is that if you value your home on the basis of its tax assessment, then the price selected is likely to be out of date and potentially less than you deserve.

PRICING IN THE REAL WORLD

So what's your home worth?

To answer this question, take these practical steps.

- Scout open houses in your neighborhood and keep detailed records of what you see.
- Speak to local real estate brokers.
- Consider the use of an appraisal up front, but only after the house is in show condition. In particular, if you can market your home to an FHA or VA buyer, you can benefit with an appropriate appraisal in hand.

Low Appraisals

If you receive an appraisal that you regard as woefully low, speak first to the appraiser—nicely. Remember, you are the homeowner and the appraiser is the professional. That does not mean the appraiser is always right, but it does mean that personalities and turf can become issues if your questions are not properly raised.

If you are *really* dismayed with the appraiser's report, then you might ask for a review by the loan underwriter. However, when sellers order an appraisal just to price a property there is no lender involved, so a field review in the usual sense is not possible.

For FHA and VA appraisals you can complain to appropriate local offices, but such appeals may not be successful or timely.

The best choice, by far, is not to have a debate. Prepare your house before it is appraised and you are likely to get a fair, and unquestionable, valuation.

- Look around. It is enormously difficult to sell a home for a price that is not reasonably consistent with the neighborhood.
- Build in a fudge factor. Pick a price that makes sense and leaves some bargaining room. Remember that asking prices and selling prices are commonly different. If your home is realistically worth $155,000 and it can be reasonably priced at $157,900 or $159,500, go for the higher value. Remember, once the home is offered for sale at $155,000, that's the highest possible price you're likely to get.
- Lastly, don't challenge reality. A home is only worth so much and the pricing of a house should be seen as a hardnosed, practical business decision.

8
Lawyers and You

Every real estate transaction comes complete with a series of potent legal issues that must be handled with great care. Title, warranties, recordation, contract language, closing, disputes, and other matters are all within the scope of the legal profession.

Lawyers are not universally loved within the real estate community, the argument of many brokers being that legal services are largely unnecessary in the marketing process, and that attorneys delay, complicate, and sometimes kill deals to justify their fees. Moreover, many brokers correctly point out that transactions in many jurisdictions are routinely handled without attorneys.

But from your perspective as a seller the issue is not brokers versus lawyers, it's taking those steps that best serve your interests. The probability is that your home is your biggest asset and selling it right is important. Hiring an attorney up front is cheap compared to the costs that may evolve if you need a lawyer after a problem develops.

As a seller you want to find an attorney prior to placing your home on the market. While brokers can handle most transactions and do so routinely, if something goes wrong a broker is not trained or licensed to give legal advice.

At the very least you want an attorney with extensive real estate experience, such as someone who handles closings and other property matters. In addition, you want an attorney who is not affiliated or recommended by your broker, someone who charges by the hour (not a percentage of the deal), and an individual you can trust.

It's probable that you will require only minimal, routine legal services, and it is equally probable that your total legal bill will amount to a few hundred dollars. Here are the areas where legal advice and counsel can be valuable.

Listing Agreements. Listing agreements tend to be short documents that establish the relationship between sellers and brokers. They are written by brokers to favor brokers, but they should be regarded as entirely open to negotiation. If you don't understand the content of a listing agreement, want something changed, or would simply like to have another set of eyes look it over, have your attorney review it before signing.

Offers. Virtually all jurisdictions have a standardized form used to arrange real estate transactions. More to the point, virtually all jurisdictions have several standardized forms, including some that may be less favorable to you as a seller than others.

Experienced, knowledgeable real estate brokers can help you review an offer in terms of such matters as price, conditions, dates, and negotiating tactics. If an offer needs to be changed, however, the rights of a broker may be limited.

In many states brokers are allowed to amend real estate contracts because such work is "incidental" to their business. Brokers in such instances commonly use form amendments to clarify issues or address special matters such as structural inspections, replacement homes, and fixtures. Some brokers also originate contract language on their own, good news when done correctly but a substantial problem if disputes arise.

In many states, however, broker rights are restricted. Brokers in some states are not allowed to complete contracts or write amendments, activities reserved for attorneys. Other states allow brokers to only complete "simple instruments." In "simple-instrument" states, brokers essentially have the right to complete form agreements (fill in the blanks).

Lawyers, then, can review offers before they are signed and add, delete, or modify language as appropriate. Since real estate agreements are common legal instruments, the cost to review and modify an offer should be minimal, especially if you are dealing with an attorney who maintains a large real estate practice. Put another way, you are not the first person to sell your home, your problems are not unique, and you are unlikely to require exotic legal forms or amendments.

Closing. You need an attorney for closing, either to conduct settlement as your representative or to review closing papers before closing.

Sellers should be aware that some attorneys who conduct closings feel they are "agents" of the settlement process and that they represent neither buyer nor seller at closing.

Why would an attorney not want to represent either a buyer or seller? In some states, lawyers who handle closings receive a commission for the sale of title insurance, sometimes 50 or 60 percent of the entire insurance premium. The fee, in addition to other charges, makes closings an attractive source of income. If an attorney represents either a buyer or seller, then collecting a fee for the sale of title insurance may well represent a conflict of interest. Thus, some attorneys prefer to act as neutral "agents."

If your attorney wants to conduct closing but does not want to represent your interests, then who does? In such situations, closing may be organized by one attorney and both seller and buyer may have separate lawyers review the papers. This may seem complicated, but there are substantial interests at risk in a real estate sale and each party should have appropriate representation.

In total, you are likely to find that legal fees for closing will cost less than the expense of a new set of drapes, substantially less if you use a legal clinic or an attorney who conducts closing on your behalf.

CUTTING LEGAL FEES

There are several steps homesellers can take to reduce legal fees.

1) Read documents before meeting with your lawyer and list specific questions. This will save time.

2) Use modern technology. An attorney can review an offer sent by fax without the expense or formality of an office visit.

3) Consider the use of a legal clinic.

4) Understand your deal with the attorney. Lawyers are in the business of selling legal services and they have a right to profit from their work, but they have no right to overcharge.

5) Shop by phone before making a commitment to one attorney or another.

6) Recognize that the practice of law involves more than form books and fancy offices. There is an art to law, a quality that makes some attorneys far better than others.

OFFERS AND CONTRACTS

With great regularity, a buyer becomes interested in a home, writes out a purchase arrangement, and suddenly everyone involved proclaims that "we have a contract." Alas, we don't.

In general terms, creating a contract is a two-step process that includes a number of conditions and tests.

To start, we first must have an offer. If Morgan says you can buy his home for $125,000, there is an offer on the table.

If Hudson says she will pay $125,000 for Morgan's house, we have acceptance and we also have a contract.

The essential calculation—offer plus acceptance equals a contract—seems fairly simple, at least until we look into some of the built-in standards that also must be met.

- The parties to the contract, the principals, must be sane and sober to be competent. We don't want to make contracts with minors because minors can withdraw unilaterally from an agreement, while adults cannot.
- There must be a mutual benefit; each side must get something.
- Contracts must be voluntary. Holding someone's knees as collateral will not meet this test.
- Both sides must understand the agreement.
- There must be "consideration" such as a deposit. Note that numbers are not important. Consideration can be $1, $100,000, or "good" consideration such as love and affection.
- A contract can only be modified with the agreement of all principals. This means that once a contract is signed it's very difficult to change.
- A contract can be withdrawn at any time before acceptance. This is why real estate brokers want offers accepted as fast as possible.
- Real estate contracts, to be enforceable, must be in writing. It is possible to have oral agreements, but not advisable.
- Real estate contracts, like other contracts, are only valid when used for legal purposes. In other words, a contract to rub out a rival gang member is not enforceable in court.

Lawyers will have a far longer list, but the basic point is this: an offer is just a piece of paper. A contract is a deal.

An offer must be accepted in full to have a contract. If there is a twenty-eight-page offer for a home and it requires the seller to include the dining-room light fixture in the sale, the entire offer is dead if this one provision—or any provision—is not accepted. Once an offer is dead, it's dead forever.

If the seller sends back the offer and accepts everything but parting with the light fixture, what we really have is a counter-offer, and a counter-offer is nothing less than a new offer. The purchaser need not accept the new offer or resurrect the old one.

Making a contract is thus an intricate dance, one that requires care, hand-holding, a good understanding of the rules, and great care to assure that no toes are stepped on.

STANDARDIZED FORMS

Visit any stationery store and you can find a good collection of standardized real estate forms. You can also find such forms in books and on electronic bulletin boards.

Such forms should each come with a large sign, in the brightest colors available, that shouts the following message: *Buyer Beware: This Form May Not Meet Local Requirements.*

Each jurisdiction has a particular set of needs and issues it feels are important. Amazing as it may seem, if you buy property in the county where I live, local regulations require that you are told of all heliports within five miles of the property. This means that local standardized contracts must have a provision where buyers acknowledge they were given such information.

Forms for use nationwide say nothing about heliports, special notices for tenants, local environmental issues, or other matters that may be important in the community where you live. And when such forms lack required information, it is possible that the entire deal may be void or voidable just because some obscure, screwball requirement has been omitted.

In this instance, at least, there is good news for sellers. Since real estate brokers have traditionally represented owner interests, every community has standardized forms that both meet local requirements and generally favor sellers.

Buried in standardized forms are dozens and dozens of significant issues that may each be addressed with a brief clause or phrase. In effect, by accepting a given form, buyers and sellers settle many issues. This can be good news, especially when the form favors one side (yours) and not the other.

Forms, then, should come from *local* brokers, attorneys, and legal clinics. In turn, if someone makes an offer on a custom-made form, or one that is not localized, look out. Your deal may be questionable and you may also find numerous "gotcha" clauses that cost both money and discomfort.

Questions to Ask

Does the attorney routinely handle real estate matters involving single-family home sales?

Does the attorney charge by the hour, as a percentage of the sale value, or a fee established in advance? If a fee is established in advance, what is included in the package and what is excluded?

How much does the attorney charge for such services, including but not limited to a review of listing agreements, purchase, offers, and closing papers?

What are the usual legal fees paid for a home sale such as yours?

If the attorney conducts closing, will you be regarded as the attorney's client?

9
Financing

If there is one joy associated with home selling, it is that owner involvement with the lending process is minimal. You don't have to apply for financing, supply reams of documentation, explain why an old credit card payment was three days late, or document the financial implications of a divorce, bankruptcy, or lawsuit.

As a seller you may sense that dealing with lenders is the buyer's problem, and that's largely true. But while you are not looking for a loan, it's very much in your interest to understand the lending system for a variety of reasons.

Take the matter of money. Your money. If a deal is financed the wrong way, you could pay thousands of dollars in excess points.

Or consider buyers. In the entire universe you need just one, but how do you know if this person can afford to buy your property? If someone makes an offer but ultimately cannot finance the deal, guess who pays mortgage expenses and property taxes each month while the sale is delayed? Or, what happens if you receive two offers that are largely alike? Which do you choose? Knowing how the lending system works can help determine your choice.

There's also your role in the marketplace. You're a seller today, but after the deal is done you're likely to become a buyer. Since your next property will probably be financed, the information gained from your home sale can not only help your purchaser, it can ultimately help when it's your turn to buy.

In many ways the best buyers of all are those who pay cash. Such purchasers are to be cherished because lender applications, approvals, and appraisals are simply unnecessary, with the result that much of the time and irritation required to close a deal are eliminated.

Who pays cash?

- Those who sold a previous home on which there was little or no debt, thus producing a large wad of cash at closing.
- People who sold a business.
- Individuals who received a buy-out when a company downsized.
- The rich and famous.
- Recent lottery winners.

Having cash, however, does not mean that buyers are willing to spend it. Many expect a discount when they buy because they can close a deal without being dependent on a lender, they can move quickly, and they do not require a seller to pay points.

While it would be very nice to find someone who both likes your home and is willing to pay for it with cash, such buyers are rare. More common are those who must deal with lenders.

CONVENTIONAL LOANS

The most basic mortgage deal, a so-called "conventional" loan, works like this: the buyer puts down 20 percent and the lender puts up the rest.

Suppose Hudson offers to buy the Clampet home for $150,000. He goes to virtually any lender and works out the following arrangement: $30,000 down and the rest ($120,000) from the lender. The loan is to be paid back over a 30-year term at a fixed rate, say 8 percent interest, or $880.52 per month for principal and interest. At the end of the loan term, the debt will be repaid in full.

Even though Hudson has $30,000 in cash to put into the deal, a solid down payment is not enough to get financing. In addition to cash, Hudson—and other buyers—need income and credit.

Let's say that it costs $400 a year to cover the cost of fire, theft, and liability insurance, and let's also say that annual taxes on your property are now set at $1,200 a year.

The basic costs of homeownership are mortgage *principal*, mortgage *interest*, property *taxes*, and property *insurance*—what lenders call "PITI."

In our example we can see that principal and interest cost $880.52 per month, property insurance is $33.33 per month ($400 divided by 12), and that taxes are $100 monthly ($1,200 divided by 12). The total cost for

How Much Can Hudson Borrow Conventionally?	
Home Price	$150,000
Down Payment	$30,000
Loan Amount	$120,000
Loan Term	30 Years
Interest Rate	8 Percent
Monthly Loan Payment	$880.52
Monthly Tax Cost	$100.00
Monthly Insurance Cost	$33.33
Total Monthly PITI	$1,013.85
Front Ratio, 28 Percent	
Required Monthly Income	$3,621.00
Required Annual Income	$43,450.00
Back Ratio, 36 Percent	
Monthly Allowance	$1,303.50
Less: PITI	($1,013.85)
Available for Debt	$289.65

PITI is $1,013.85.

A conventional lender will allow borrowers to devote as much as 28 percent of their gross annual income to PITI. Knowing this, we can divide $1,013.85 by 28 to come up with $36.21, an amount equal to 1 percent of the gross monthly income Hudson needs. If we take $36.21 and multiply by 100, we can see that Hudson needs a gross monthly income of $3,621 to qualify for his loan, or a total income of $43,450 annually.

We have just looked at Hudson's "front" ratio and you can guess that where there is a front ratio there must be a "back" one as well.

A conventional lender wants to be certain that Hudson has enough income to pay not only for homeownership costs but also for other debts such as car payments, credit-card bills, student loans, and other fixed expenses. To figure out how much Hudson can pay out each month, a conventional lender will allow the back ratio to equal 36 percent of Hudson's gross income.

(The front and back ratios have evolved into a kind of shorthand that lenders use when qualifying borrowers. If you ask about ratios for a conventional loan, a lender will say they are "28/36," meaning 28 percent is the front ratio and 36 percent is the back ratio.)

We know that Hudson needs an income of at least $43,450 to underwrite PITI. If we take 36 percent of $43,450, it comes out to $15,642 per year or $1,303.50 a month. Subtract PITI, $1,013.85, and there is $289.65 left over for monthly debts.

In addition to front and back ratios, a lender will also want to verify certain data before putting up the $128,000 sought by Hudson.

- Does Hudson pay his bills?

Having income is great, but people who make money but don't pay their bills, or don't pay on time, are poor credit risks. Either they don't get loans or they pay a higher interest rate for the financing they obtain. To assure creditworthiness, lenders will obtain a complete credit report.

- Where does Hudson get his money?

In the usual case, lenders would like Hudson to have worked at least two years in the same field. To verify employment, lenders will want W-2 forms for the past two years, as well as original payroll stubs for the last 30 days. For those who are self-employed, a lender will want tax returns for the past two or three years.

- What is the property worth?

In the last chapter we looked at appraisals, and now is the time when such evaluations are required. An appraiser acceptable to the lender (but paid for by the borrower) will go out to the property and create a complete written estimate of value.

The lender uses an appraisal (two if the property is sufficiently expensive) to assure that the property exists and that it's worth the selling price. The difference between the market value and the loan amount is the cushion needed by the lender for protection in case Hudson fails to pay off the loan.

If the appraiser agrees that the Hudson property is worth $150,000 and the lender puts up $120,000, then in case of default the property can be sold at foreclosure for far less than $150,000 without hurting the lender. For instance, if the loan has an outstanding balance of $115,000 when the loan is defaulted and foreclosure costs are $5,000, then the property can be sold for $120,000 and the lender won't lose a dime.

One further catch with regard to conventional loans: each year a limit is placed on the size of a conventional mortgage. As an example, in 1993 the limit was $203,150. If your buyer wants to borrow above the conventional limit, then a "jumbo" loan will be required, a mortgage with a somewhat higher rate than conventional financing because a bigger loan implies a bigger risk.

ARMS

In the example with buyer Hudson, we saw how he could buy with fixed-rate, conventional financing. Another alternative that Hudson might consider is the adjustable-rate mortgage, or ARM.

With an ARM the initial interest rate—or "teaser" rate—is sometimes 3 percent lower than fixed-rate interest levels. However, after the first six months or a year, the rate can change.

Most ARMs—but not all—provide that *rates* can rise or fall as much as 2 percent per year, say from 7 percent to 9 percent. The monthly *payment* can rise or fall 7.5 percent, so—for example—the monthly cost for principal and interest can go from $800 one year to as much as $860 the next.

How the rate changes, and how much, depends on two factors.

Each ARM is tied to an index, say the movement of the one-year trea-

How Much Can Hudson Borrow with an ARM?	
Home Price	$150,000
Down Payment	$30,000
Loan Amount	$120,000
Loan Term	30 Years
Start Rate	5 Percent
Initial Monthly Payment	$644.19
Monthly Tax Cost	$100.00
Monthly Insurance Cost	$33.33
Total Monthly PITI	$777.52
Qualifying Interest Rate	7 Percent
Qualifying Monthly Payment	$798.36
Monthly Tax Cost	$100.00
Monthly Insurance Cost	$33.33
Total Qualifying PITI	$931.69
Front Ratio, 28 Percent	
Required Monthly Income	$3,327.46
Required Annual Income	$39,929.57
Back Ratio, 36 Percent	
Monthly Allowance	$1,197.89
Less: PITI	($931.69)
Available for Debt	$266.20

sury securities of the ups and downs associated with the popular—and slow-moving—11th District cost-of-funds index that relates to loans made in California, Arizona, and Nevada but which is used for loans nationwide.

A fixed "margin" is then added to the index rate to come up with a final interest level. For example, if the margin is 2.5 and the index is at 4.5, the interest rate is 7 percent. If the margin is at 2.5 percent and the index falls to 3.5 percent, the borrower will have a 6 percent rate.

Qualifying for ARMs is sometimes easier than with fixed-rate loans. Conventional ARMs use 28/36 ratios, but so-called "nonconforming" ARM products often use 33/38 ratios.

Borrowers often need less income to qualify for an ARM, because a hidden standard is buried in the ARM qualification process.

The ability of a borrower to finance a home is based in part on how much monthly income can be used for PITI. Lenders look at income, monthly PITI costs, and other credit expenses, and then determine if a borrower has enough money to qualify for a loan.

With ARMs the evaluation process is a little different. If lenders qualified buyers on the basis of the low introductory interest rate, then there would be a large number of foreclosures the moment rates rise. To protect against rising interest costs, lenders typically qualify prospects on the basis of the first-anniversary rate or a baseline interest level—whichever is higher.

To see how this works, imagine that Hudson's ARM starts out at 5 percent interest for one year. The loan can rise by as much as 2 percent a year, so the top rate in year two will be 7 percent.

If Hudson borrows $120,000 with an initial interest rate of 5 percent interest over 30 years, his monthly cost for principal and interest will total $644.19. Add $100 a month for taxes and $33.33 for insurance, and total PITI in this example is $777.52. If the front ratio is 28 percent, Hudson needs just $2,776.86 a month to qualify for financing, or $33,322.29 a year.

But if Hudson is qualified at the 7 percent rate, matters change. Now the monthly cost for principal and interest is $798.36 and the total PITI is $931.69. Using the 28 percent front ratio, Hudson needs $39,929.57 to qualify with ARM financing—about $4,000 a year less income than a fixed-rate borrower.

FHA BASICS

The conventional loan used by Hudson was distinguished by a big down payment up front and conservative qualifying ratios. Not everyone has so much cash, especially first-time buyers who have not had enough time to build up savings.

We could, as a nation, simply require first-time buyers to spend years accumulating enough cash to pay 20 percent down for a home, but that would hurt us all. The marketplace needs first-time buyers because such purchasers typically acquire entry-level homes. The people who *sell* entry-level homes then move up, creating a market for properties in the middle-price ranges. Some of the people who sell middle-price homes retire to smaller properties or buy mansions and estates.

Activity in the real estate market thus resembles a primordial food chain of sorts. Sharks don't eat shrimp and kelp, but shrimp and kelp are needed for the smaller fish that represent the shark's dinner. In a similar manner, those who sell middle-income properties and even great mansions ultimately rely on first-time buyers to power the market.

While some doomsayers worry that population growth is declining and with it the supply of first-time buyers, population alone does not determine housing demand. A more important trend is the pace of household formations, and that trend—according to Census Bureau figures—shows that we are forming households at a far greater pace than we are building housing units. The result is more demand than supply, and a huge backlog of potential homebuyers.

Okay, so there are lots of first-time buyers out there, but most lack the 20 percent down needed to buy a house. We need to convert such individuals into solid prospects, and the best way to do that is to create deals that require less than 20 percent down.

One approach that has worked for millions of homebuyers has been financing guaranteed by the Federal Housing Administration (FHA).

There are no FHA loans in the sense that you can go to a government office and pick up a check. Instead, the FHA guarantees to repay loans made by commercial lenders, a guarantee that greatly limits lender risk.

With FHA financing, the down payment is equal to 3 percent of the first $25,000 borrowed, 5 percent of the next $100,000, and 10 percent of everything higher—a far lower down payment than conventional loans require. In addition, the FHA program has more liberal qualification standards than conventional financing. Instead of 28/36 qualifying ratios, an FHA borrower can qualify with a front ratio of 29 percent and a back ratio of 41 percent.

For Hudson, our model buyer, the FHA program offers several advantages.

First, Hudson needs fewer dollars to buy a home.

Hudson, our buyer, wants a home priced at $150,000. With conventional financing he needs $30,000 up front for a down payment, but with FHA backing Hudson needs $8,250 (3 percent × $25,000 = $750, 5 percent × $100,000 = $5,000, and 10 percent × $25,000 = $2,500).

A lower down payment is certainly good news, but in home buying—like physics—for every action there is an equal and opposite reaction.

Because the down payment is lower, there is more to borrow. With an FHA-backed loan, Hudson trades a lower down payment for a bigger loan and larger monthly payments.

Second, with FHA financing the larger loan amount is offset with more liberal qualification standards.

We know that PITI will cost $1,173.44 each month. With a 29 percent front ratio, Hudson must earn $4,046.35 per month ($1,173.44 divided by 29 and then multiplied by 100), or $48,556.19 per year. That's more income than Hudson would need for a conventional loan, but if Hudson is like many people he has income but not savings.

As to the back ratio, with the conventional loan Hudson can qualify for financing if his monthly debts were less than $289.65 per month. With FHA, the back ratio is 41 percent and Hudson can have monthly debts of as much as $485.56 and still get financing.

Third, with an FHA loan Hudson can cut settlement expenses by financing many closing costs over the loan term. In effect, rather than needing vast wads of cash up front, Hudson can pay out closing costs over many years by obtaining a somewhat larger loan.

The FHA program is ideal for entry-level buyers because it's nationwide, easy to understand, requires little money up front, and uses more liberal qualification standards that make homes more affordable.

Sellers, however, should be aware of two factors that make FHA financing less than ideal.

One limitation is that FHA financing is capped. Buyers can only borrow so much, $151,725 at this time for a single-family residence in high-cost urban areas. The maximum amounts available in many areas are significantly below the big-city threshold, which means that FHA financing will not work for many sellers. (In Alaska, Hawaii, and Guam, maximum FHA loan amounts are higher than in the continental United States.)

A second matter concerns fees. The FHA program is an insurance plan, funded by buyers. At this time there is an up-front fee equal to 3 percent of

How Much Can Hudson Borrow with FHA Financing?	
Home Price	$150,000
Down Payment	$8,250
Loan Amount	$141,750
Loan Term	30 Years
Interest Rate	8 Percent
Monthly Loan Payment	$1,040.11
Monthly Tax Cost	$100.00
Monthly Insurance Cost	$33.33
Total Monthly PITI	$1,173.44
Front Ratio, 29 Percent	
Required Monthly Income	$4,046.35
Required Annual Income	$48,556.19
Back Ratio, 41 Percent	
Monthly Allowance	$1,659.00
Less: PITI	($1,173.44)
Available for Debt	$485.56

the loan amount, and there is also an annual premium equal to 0.5 percent of the outstanding mortgage balance. The good news is that the up-front premium is scheduled to decline in 1995 and, regardless, it can be financed over the loan term. In effect, the up-front fee need not be up front.

In addition to the basic FHA program [203(b)] described here, there are a variety of FHA plans for owner-occupied, two- to four-unit properties, as well as for homes that need extensive repair.

VA LOANS

Virtually all buyers have access to FHA financing, but a second government program is more restrictive—and more interesting.

VA financing, now operated by the Department of Veterans Affairs (DVA), rewards military personnel and certain other individuals such as reservists and national-guard personnel who have served at least six years.

With the VA there is no down-payment requirement, most lenders will allow as much as $184,000 to be borrowed under the VA program at this time, and the qualifying ratios are sky-high at 41/41. There is no annual insurance premium, and—instead of the hefty up-front charges associated with FHA financing—there is currently a "funding fee" of 2 percent of the loan amount, or less, depending on how much is put down.

How Much Can Hudson Borrow with VA Financing?	
Home Price	$150,000
Down Payment	$0
Loan Amount	$150,000
Loan Term	30 Years
Interest Rate	8 Percent
Monthly Loan Payment	$1,100.65
Monthly Tax Cost	$100.00
Monthly Insurance Cost	$33.33
Total Monthly PITI	$1,233.98
Front Ratio, 41 Percent	
Required Monthly Income	$3,009.70
Required Annual Income	$36,116.40
Back Ratio, 41 Percent	
Monthly Allowance	$1,233.98
Less: PITI	($1,233.98)
Available for Debt	$0

To sell with VA financing you need a qualified individual who has form DD214, a certification that someone has sufficient federal service to qualify for the VA program. You will also need a VA-approved appraisal, which can be obtained through a lender. Otherwise, the borrowing process is much like a conventional loan.

MORTGAGE BONDS AND CERTIFICATES

If you sell an entry-level property to a first-time buyer, then it may be possible for your purchaser to finance the deal with a mortgage through a state or local government.

In basic terms, government funding can work in two ways. One choice is to borrow money from the public through the sale of bonds. Since the government has a good credit record, it pays less interest than a commercial lender or an individual.

Money collected from the bond sale is then made available in the form of mortgage financing for local buyers. Since the bonds have a low interest rate, the government can pass on low interest costs to homebuyers.

Because bonds are issued by the state, the interest paid to investors is tax deductible. Thus state bonds are effectively subsidized by the federal government because investors can reduce tax payments to Uncle Sam.

And since the federal government does not want an endless supply of tax-free bonds in circulation, it creates an allocation for each state based on population.

As an alternative to bonds, states may issue mortgage credit certificates (MCCs). MCCs also take money out of the federal treasury, but in a manner somewhat different from bonds.

With MCCs, a buyer obtains financing from a regular lender as well as certificates from the state. A purchaser, for example, may receive a certificate that allows 20 percent of all mortgage interest to be taken as an income tax credit.

If Wilson has a $40,000 mortgage and pays out interest worth $3,200, then under an MCC program he might be allowed to claim a tax credit of 20 percent, or $640 in this case. The other 80 percent of his interest bill, $2,560, would be written off as an itemized deduction for mortgage interest.

The value of Wilson's tax credit may be nothing if he has little income and many deductions. Alternatively, if Wilson is in the 15 percent bracket, then a $640 tax credit is equal to untaxed income worth $4,266.

To obtain bond-backed financing, purchasers must not exceed income limitations or have owned property for at least three years. There are other qualifications as well, so if you are marketing an entry-level property be certain to speak with brokers, lenders, and local officials for complete details.

PRIVATE MORTGAGE INSURANCE

We know that buyers need 20 percent down to finance a home with a conventional mortgage, and we also know they need far less if they use FHA, VA, or state-backed financing. But what happens to the buyer who wants a home yet cannot use governmental programs?

This is a common problem because many buyers are not VA-qualified or earn too much for state-backed loans. Additionally, the FHA mortgage limit makes that program unusable in many areas, especially high-cost metropolitan regions.

Private mortgage insurance (MI) has been developed to help such buyers with a trade-off that works this way: in exchange for the buyer paying a premium, an insurance company promises a lender that if the property must be foreclosed, the lender will get back most or all of its money.

With the backing of an insurance company, the buyer no longer needs 20 percent down. Deals with 5 percent, 10 percent, or 15 percent up front are entirely possible.

Sounds good, but there are—as you may suspect—a few considerations to keep in mind.

First, there is the little matter of monthly payments. Suppose Morley is buying a $185,000 home. With 20 percent down our buyer needs $37,000 up front, plus closing costs. Using mortgage insurance, however, Morley can buy with as little as 5 percent down, or $9,250—a cash reduction of $27,750.

But if Morley puts less down, he must borrow more. That means he must be able to qualify for new and larger mortgage amounts. It also means Morley must pay more each month to own his home.

If Morley borrows $148,000 ($185,000 less 20 percent) at 8.5 percent interest over 30 years, he will have monthly principal and interest costs of $1,137.99. If he puts down just 5 percent, then he must borrow $175,750. With 8.5 percent financing he will pay $1,351.37 per month for 30 years.

Premiums are the second issue raised by MI. Borrowers can have a lump-sum payment up front—what the industry calls a single premium—or an annual premium. Nineteen of 20 buyers will opt for annual payments, and unless you have an excruciating desire to explore the complexities of private mortgage insurance, simply tell would-be buyers that they may be able to buy your home with as little as 5 percent down. As to the details, have their lender explain how private mortgage insurance works.

ASSUMPTIONS AND FINANCING "SUBJECT TO"

When you bought your home, the probability is that you obtained financing, financing that may now evolve into a useful sales tool.

A mortgage is potentially more than a loan to you. It may also become a loan *for your buyer* if it is "assumed" or if the property is sold "subject to" the mortgage.

Suppose Robertson wants to sell his home for $115,000 and his current loan balance is $93,000. Wendt, a would-be buyer, sees the property and makes this offer: $15,000 in cash plus assumption of the loan, a total of $108,000 for the property.

Granted, $108,000 is less than the $115,000, but Robertson is not being asked to pay points, a buyer is in hand, and no one bid $115,000 anyway. Once the home is sold, Wendt will continue to make the monthly payments that Robinson would have made until the debt is paid off or assumed by someone else.

So far, we have a quick and easy example of an assumption, but as you might guess, in real life things have a habit of becoming more complex.

Let us start with Robertson's assumable loan. For the past decade or so, most loans have not been freely assumable. "Freely assumable" is a magical phrase that means a buyer can take over the loan whether the lender likes it or not, regardless of the buyer's financial qualifications and credit history.

Lenders don't like loans that are freely assumable, so now they largely make loans that have a due-on-sale clause or a clause allowing qualified assumptions.

With a due-on-sale clause the loan term is "accelerated" if the property is sold. In English, this means if you sell, the lender can demand that you pay off the loan at closing.

A clause allowing qualified assumptions works somewhat differently. Here the lender says that it may be possible to assume the loan, but only if the borrower meets the lender's standards. Such standards may include appropriate income, credit, and the willingness to pay an assumption fee. Alternatively, a lender may set assumption standards so high that as a practical matter the loan is not assumable at all.

In the case of FHA mortgages the situation is somewhat different. Loans made before December 14, 1989, are freely assumable; FHA loans made after December 15, 1989, can only be assumed by qualified owner–occupants—investors need not bother.

With VA financing, the situation looks like this: loans made before March 1, 1988, are freely assumable; those made after March 1, 1988, can only be assumed by a qualified borrower.

Assumable financing, especially loans that are freely assumable, can make your home more salable in several situations.

- When you assume a loan after several years, more of the payment is principal than in the first years. The result is a better mix of interest and principal.
- If the interest rate on your loan is below current market levels, buyers are getting bargain financing. This means you can sometimes get a better price than might otherwise be possible.
- Your home can be sold to marginal buyers. As an example, if Conklin went bankrupt several years ago, he may have a tough time getting a mortgage, depending on why he went bankrupt and what has hap-

pened since then. With a freely assumable mortgage, Conklin can buy a home—perhaps yours—regardless of past problems.

When a home is sold with assumable financing it does not mean the seller is free and clear of all obligation to repay the debt. What happens is that the new owner has the *primary* obligation to repay, but if the new borrower does not make good on the loan, the lender can come after the homeseller who originally took out the mortgage.

How much risk is there with assumed financing? It depends on several factors.

One issue is how much cash the buyer is putting into the property. More cash (or a second trust held by someone other than you) equals less owner risk.

A second factor concerns the marketplace. If home prices are rising, then the difference between the loan amount and the market price is widening—good news for homesellers who have allowed assumptions.

But if home prices are falling, or the buyer wants a deal with no money down, then it's seller beware. The potential for disaster is greatly increased because your financial fate is tied to a plunging asset and a buyer who may or may not have the ability to make payments.

While qualified assumptions are not as good a deal as mortgages that are freely assumable, there is considerable sense to the notion that buyers ought to be qualified before allowed to assume a loan. The qualification process—if reasonable—protects the seller as well as the lender because the buyer must have the financial wherewithal to make the deal work.

Even in those cases where freely assumable financing is available, sellers should require full financial disclosure before a deal is finalized. *Know your buyer is good advice, especially when you may be on the hook after the deal is done.*

Selling a home "subject to" the mortgage is much like selling with an assumption. There is one substantial difference, but it's a gem.

With an assumption, if something goes wrong the first person the lender will chase is the buyer. But when a home is sold "subject to" the mortgage, the arrangement is different. The buyer simply has no liability to the lender, and you can bet that if the buyer has no liability, someone else must. And that someone, of course, is you.

If something goes wrong with a deal where the buyer bought "subject to" the mortgage, the purchaser will lose the property and such equity as he or she has in it. Whatever value the property has will be used to offset the mortgage debt, and if there is not enough to repay the loan and assorted foreclosure costs, a lender will want to discuss your obligations at some length.

The bottom line looks like this: buyers with cash and credit should be seen as potential assumption candidates. Purchasers who want to buy "subject to" the loan should be required to make a significant capital infusion into the property, the more the better.

SECOND TRUSTS

When real estate is financed there is a pecking order of sorts regarding the fundamental question of who gets paid first if something goes wrong. The pecking order goes like this: the first debt on record is the first paid, the second recorded debt is the second paid, and on and on.

The business of who gets paid first is not just a symbolic matter, because there is also another consideration involved. In a foreclosure, the first debt must be paid completely before the second debt is paid, and the second debt must be completely paid off before the third obligation can be addressed, and so forth.

The bottom line is that as a lender you want to hold the first trust or first mortgage because you have less risk than other lenders further back in line. Seen the other way, more risk means higher interest rates.

Second trusts can be provided by lenders, by third-party sources, and by sellers. As an illustration, if Mr. Hampton is buying a home for $200,000, he might obtain a first trust worth $160,000 at 7 percent interest and a seven-year, $20,000 second trust at 9 percent.

Or, perhaps Hampton can put down $20,000, assume an existing loan for $150,000 at 7 percent, and obtain a second trust for $30,000.

Unlike first trusts, second trusts tend to have shorter loan terms (say three to 10 years rather than 30), higher interest rates, and monthly payments based on 30-year schedules. To see why 30-year schedules are used, look at the deal with Mr. Hampton.

Hampton is borrowing $20,000 for a period of seven years at 9 percent. To pay off the loan completely within the loan term, his cost will total $321.78 per month. However, if he uses a 30-year payment schedule, his monthly cost will drop to $160.92—an expense that is more tolerable.

The only problem with the lower monthly payments is that Hampton's second trust doesn't have a 30-year term. Since the loan will only last seven years, a large part of the debt will remain, $18,728.63 to be exact in this example.

Lenders may or may not allow the use of second trusts when a home is purchased, depending on the amount paid down by the buyer, the buyer's financial qualifications, and the lender's policies with regard to individual loan programs. Thus a second trust should be seen as a potent financial tool, but not one that can be used in all cases.

10
Sellers as Lenders

So far, the universe of buyers has been occupied by those who pay cash and those who borrow from traditional lenders. There is a third group as well: those who look for you—the seller—to finance the deal, or at least a part of it.

If ever the expression "watch your wallet" has importance, now is the moment. Seller financing is a perfectly legitimate concept that has been distorted and convulsed in recent years by the get-rich-quick, no-money-down gurus who peddle an instant-wealth theology to the greedy and desperate. If you're not careful, you could wind up as both a seller and a victim by dealing with such folks on their terms.

A home is a commodity that most people cannot possibly buy for cash. Given a capital shortage, it follows that people must borrow, and that explains why the phone books are filled with lenders.

While we usually think of "lenders" as bankers or mortgage brokers, there is no rule that says you cannot finance the sale of your property and, in fact, there's much to recommend such an approach.

Suppose Rollins has a home on which there is no debt. Rollins might offer his property for $100,000 and the deal could work this way. Buyer Shubert comes along, puts down $20,000, and Rollins lends—or "takes back"—an $80,000 mortgage with interest at 8 percent, a fair rate at the time of sale.

When it's time to close, Rollins will receive $20,000 in cash (less closing costs) and a note, or I.O.U., for $80,000 will be recorded as a first trust in local land records.

The Rollins deal makes sense for both buyer and seller. The seller need not worry about lender approvals, inspections, and underwriting standards. The buyer is putting down 20 percent in cash, enough money to limit the risk associated with Rollins's loan. And, also, there is the matter of 8 percent interest from the note, a stream of income that may be better than anything Rollins might obtain elsewhere.

Buyer Shubert should also be happy. The Rollins loan is at a fair rate and there are no points to pay. Mountains of paperwork are not required and the entire deal can be quickly completed.

If Rollins is selling his home in a down market, or if he wants to maximize his price, he might offer a lower rate to attract buyers, say 7 percent financing. His home will be more affordable than competing properties, which means he will have a larger pool of buyers. At the same time, his asking price will be more acceptable because it includes discounted financing.

Alas, owner financing is not always as neat and clean as the deal between Rollins and Shubert.

In the example used here we have a home that is free and clear of debt, a seller who does not need cash from the sale of his property to buy a next home, a buyer with 20 percent down, and loan documents that have been recorded as a first trust.

Ask yourself a question: how likely is such a scenario?

Most homes have debt at the time of sale, debt that is in the form of a first trust or a first mortgage. This debt must either be paid off, assumed, or the property must be sold subject to the existing mortgage. But not all loans are assumable and selling a home subject to the mortgage is not always a good idea (see previous chapter).

A more likely deal with seller financing works like this: Pickens has a property worth $100,000. There is an assumable first trust with a $75,000 mortgage balance and Pickens offers to take back a $25,000 second trust.

The Pickens deal is a classic sale with no money down. Whether it's also a good idea is an open question.

If someone takes the Pickens offer, then the situation will look like this:

- The house will be "sold," an important consideration if Pickens must move or the local market is weak.
- Pickens will receive no money at closing.
- Pickens will own a note secured by the property. The note will be worth $25,000 and will produce a stream of income.
- The buyer will have 100 percent financing. No cash, other than closing costs, will be required at settlement.

- The buyer will have the largest possible payments because 100 percent of the purchase price is being financed.

If the buyer is a great and wonderful person, the Pickens deal is workable. But if the buyer defaults, then huge problems can arise.

Pickens owns a second trust. If he is not paid, he can move to have the property foreclosed. But wait. If the property is foreclosed, then the first-trust lender must be *completely* repaid before any money can be used to pay off Pickens. If the property sells at foreclosure for $85,000, then the first-trust lender will receive $75,000 and Pickens will only get $10,000.

So while it's true that Pickens can foreclose, he may not gain much benefit by calling the loan. Pickens, to a very real extent, is a financial hostage if something goes wrong.

If Pickens's second trust is not repaid, he can live with it, hope for repayment, or foreclose. But if the first-trust lender is not paid, matters are worse. The first-trust lender has no interest in the property other than the balance of the first trust—$75,000 in this case. If the buyer fails to make payments on the first trust, then that lender can foreclose and Pickens is, once again, in trouble.

Because they entail more risk, second trusts usually command more interest. That's fine, except when interest rates are generally high.

If interest rates are sufficiently steep they may bump into state usury laws—rules that limit interest levels. If a loan violates a usury law, then it's possible for a lender to lose the right to collect all interest and suffer other penalties—as if losing all interest is not sufficient penalty.

WRAPAROUND LOANS

We have looked at first trusts and second trusts from sellers, but there is an interesting loan alternative for sellers, the so-called wraparound mortgage.

Monroe has a home to sell with a freely assumable loan of $25,000 at 6 percent. Current loan rates are pegged at 9 percent, so Monroe offers this deal: he'll sell his home for $120,000 and provide wraparound financing worth $100,000 at 9 percent. Buyer Jenkins comes along, likes the deal, and the sale is done.

At closing, the Monroe sale looks like this: Jenkins puts up $20,000 in cash. Monroe creates a loan worth $100,000 and agrees to repay the existing first trust over time. In return for creating a wraparound loan, Monroe receives 9 percent interest.

A careful look at this arrangement shows that Monroe did very well. He has not actually put up the $25,000 needed to repay the existing first trust. Instead, he pays the first-trust lender 6 percent while collecting 9 percent from Jenkins. That's a 3 percent difference or roughly $2,250 in the first year.

Monroe also gets 9 percent on the $25,000 credit he has given buyer Jenkins.

If we add the 3 percent Monroe is earning on the first trust ($2,250) and the 9 percent he's receiving on the second trust ($2,250), his return for putting up $25,000 is roughly $4,500 in the first year of the loan—a return of 18 percent annually.

For sellers with freely assumable financing it can pay to suggest wraparound financing rather than a deal that allows the buyer to simply assume an existing first trust. Speak to a local real estate attorney for the paperwork needed to make a wraparound work in your community.

LAND CONTRACTS

Land contracts are an arrangement where there is a lender and a borrower. The catch is that unlike other forms of financing, with a land con-

Mr. Monroe's Wraparound Mortgage	
Sale Price	$120,000
Down Payment	$20,000
Loan Amount	$100,000
Existing First Trust	$75,000
Credit from Monroe to the Buyer	$25,000
Total Financing	$100,000
Overall Interest Rate	9 Percent
Interest on Existing First Trust	6 Percent
Interest Differential	3 Percent
Cash Differential	$2,250
Interest on Monroe Credit	9 percent
Cash Flow ($25,000 × 9 percent)	$2,250
Cash Differential from First Trust	$2,250
Total Cash Flow	$4,500
Amount Loaned by Monroe	$25,000
Interest Generated by Loan	$4,500
True Rate of Return	18 Percent

tract the buyer does not actually hold title until some or all of the loan has been repaid.

Suppose Wirthlin offers to sell his property for $180,000 with a land contract—also known as a *contract for deed*, an *installment sale*, or a *conditional sales agreement*. The buyer will make monthly payments to Wirthlin and then, when a certain number of payments are made (or when all payments are made), title will be given over to the purchaser.

Land contracts give tremendous leverage to sellers. Much like an installment sale for a refrigerator, if a borrower misses a single payment it becomes possible to take back the property. There is no worry about foreclosure because the buyer has no title, only an "equitable" interest in the property.

But although land contracts are the most pro-seller form of financing one can imagine, they are not without problems.

1) If the property is now financed, current lenders may see a land contract as evidence of a sale. If there is a due-on-sale clause or if the buyer must be qualified to assume the loan, expect big problems from the lender.

2) Land contracts raise insurance problems. Who carries fire, theft, and liability insurance—the owner or the buyer? Who collects if the house burns down? Who is responsible if a letter carrier slips on the front walk? (Note that lenders sometimes find out about land contracts when they see that the property insurance is held by someone other than the owner.)

3) What are the borrower's rights? Can he or she sell the property? Get a second trust? Refinance?

4) Can the installment loan be prepaid? Is there a grace period for late payments?

5) What happens if the buyer/borrower doesn't make a payment and doesn't want to move? He or she is not a tenant in the usual sense so an eviction may be difficult or impossible. Then again, if the buyer/borrower is a tenant it's possible that rent control regulations may apply to the property.

DISCOUNTS AND PREMIUMS

Seller financing can be attractive if you want to create a stream of income or as a device to make a property more salable. However, owners should understand that the face value of a loan is unlikely to be a full measure of its worth.

Suppose Hamilton has a $35,000 interest-only note from the sale of a home and an interest rate of 9 percent. Suppose as well that the only people who will buy such a note seek 11 percent interest. In such an event, Hamilton must sell his note with a discounted face value if he needs cash.

To measure the value of Hamilton's loan, we can look at his rate of return. He receives 9 percent per year, or $3,150 the first year. If $3,150 equals an 11 percent rate of return, then the cash value of Hamilton's loan is $28,636 ($3,150 divided by 11 × 100).

Conversely, it's possible for Hamilton to actually sell his note for more than the face value. If the $35,000 note has a 9 percent interest rate and interest levels for second trusts fall to 8 percent, then Hamilton can get a premium for his note. He has an annual income of $3,150 from the loan and at 8 percent his note is worth $39,375 ($3,150 divided by 8 × 100)—if he can find a buyer.

NO-MONEY-DOWNERS

To make matters worse for sellers, we have a large number of individuals who have read the books, listened to the tapes, and attended the seminars where they have been told how to make millions in real estate even if they lack such fundamentals as cash, credit, or a job.

No problem, say the no-money-down gurus. Find a home with assumable financing. Have the owner—you—take back a second trust so no money down is required for the deal. Have the owner pay closing costs. Buy at a price 20 to 25 percent below prevailing market values. Avoid real estate brokers and attorneys.

Where do you find an owner willing to make such a deal? Look for a "flexible" seller—someone getting divorced or who has financial troubles. After all, honorable no-money-downers, it is claimed, are merely preserving the credit ratings of solid citizens who have fallen on hard times. Sure.

The jackpot for a no-money-downer works like this: not only does the seller take back financing and pay all closing costs but the deal is rigged up front with several "gotcha" clauses.

For instance, the financing may include a "subordination" clause, legal language that says while you are taking back a second trust, the buyer has the right to borrow more and to push your loan behind such additional financing. In other words, your second trust can mutate into a third trust or perhaps even a fourth trust. If you think there are risks with a second trust, imagine the thrill of holding a fourth trust in a foreclosure situation.

Then there is the "substitution" clause. This gem says that you, the seller/lender, give the borrower the right to substitute your loan's collateral. In other words, instead of having a loan secured by real estate, the borrower can use other assets to secure the loan—say another piece of property. Or a boat. Or "artwork." Whether or not the new collateral is worth as much as the property, or is as salable, are questions sellers should seek to avoid.

HOW TO PROTECT YOUR INTERESTS

There is little doubt that seller financing is a plausible and sometimes attractive device to market real estate. Whether it is workable in your particular situation is an open question, but before offering to take back a loan, here are several steps to consider.

1) *Never take back financing unless the buyer is willing to put cash into the deal.* Unlike commercial lenders who want either 20 percent down or insurance to protect their interest, as a seller/lender you are unlikely to obtain such a large down payment and you do not have access to outside loan guarantees. A down payment of at least 10 percent should be required.

2) If you are the lender, you have a right to all the information a commercial lender would normally receive. Tax returns, credit reports, and verifications from employers and landlords should be required.

3) There should be no requirement to take back a loan unless you are *satisfied* with the buyer information you receive.

4) *Never take back financing without adequate legal counsel.* You should obtain the services of a knowledgeable local attorney to review any purchase offer that requires seller financing, *before you sign anything.*

5) You should have your attorney prepare all loan documents so that they are consistent with local rules and regulations—and so your interests are fully protected.

6) Your loan should be immediately recorded at the time of closing.

7) If you are considering the use of owner financing, speak first to a CPA, tax attorney, or enrolled agent. What are the tax implications of seller financing? How should interest from your loan be reported? How are profits determined and reported?

8) If you are considering the use of a land contract, first speak with a local real estate attorney to determine what is appropriate in your situation.

9) If you want to use wraparound financing, make certain that the

deal is first reviewed by a local real estate attorney to assure that you have the right to continue the old loan and to guarantee that your loan papers are properly prepared.

10) Never take back financing where the borrower has the right to subordinate your loan, where your collateral can be substituted, where the buyer puts up little or no cash, or where the borrower provides the loan documents.

11
Marketing Your Home

Regardless of the merit an individual property may offer, without marketing there is only one word to describe it: unsold.

To sell property you must get the word out to as many people as possible. You only need one buyer, but the odds of finding that one special person improve with each additional individual who hears about your property.

While no one can guarantee the sale of real estate in the open marketplace, there is no doubt that marketing helps. And good marketing starts not with an ad or a sign but with an analysis of what you are selling.

It is entirely possible that you already know who will buy your home—not by name, but by profile. It is this profile that can be used to *target* your marketing efforts.

Consider the Robinson home. It's priced at $240,000. Clearly not a starter home, it's likely that this property will be purchased by a current homeowner. According to figures developed by the National Association of Realtors, that means the buyer is likely to place 25 percent down and finance the rest—a deal with $60,000 up front and a loan valued at $180,000.

With our probable profile in mind, we know that the house is unlikely to attract an FHA borrower (the FHA loan limit means a buyer would put down more than 35 percent, not a likely scenario). A high-income VA borrower is possible, someone with the capacity to get VA financing worth as much as $184,000. Most VA loans, however, involve much smaller loan amounts, so a VA buyer is not plausible.

Since our buyers are likely to put down 25 percent, they will not require private mortgage insurance. They can go for a conventional fixed-rate loan, or they can buy with an ARM. If interest rates are set at 8.5 percent, and if property taxes and insurance cost $225 per month, then we can estimate the income needed to buy the property.

A 30-year, $180,000 mortgage at 8.5 percent will require monthly payments of $1,384.04 per month. Add on $200 per month for taxes and an insurance cost of $40 monthly, and the total monthly expense for principal, interest, taxes, and insurance (PITI) will be $1,624.04.

We know that a conventional loan will allow borrowers to devote as much as 28 percent of their income to PITI. If $1,624.04 equals 28 percent of monthly household income, then the total income is $5,800 per month, or $69,600 yearly.

If ARM financing is used, then some liberal programs will allow as much as 33 percent of gross household income for use as PITI.

We can expect a low start rate, say 5.5 percent, and we can also expect a higher qualifying rate, perhaps 7.5 percent. If someone borrows $180,000 at 7.5 percent over 30 years, the monthly cost for principal and interest will total $1,258.59. Add taxes ($200) and insurance ($40), and the monthly PITI totals $1,498.59.

If the buyer uses a liberal ARM, then an income of $4,541.18 a month, or $54,494.18 will be required to buy the property—assuming the home sells at full price and the buyer is not burdened with a large pile of monthly debts.

Given our projections, the Robinson home can be marketed as a move-up opportunity. We can tout tax deductions that make the property more affordable, and we can consider owner financing for a qualified buyer with 25 percent down.

We are likely to be dealing with someone who has had time to accumulate equity and possessions, and so we should emphasize space, storage, and entertaining. Location relative to employment zones such as downtown office cores and suburban centers should be noted.

The availability of schools, shopping, and religious centers should be regarded as obvious, unless such facilities are exceptional or unique.

The same analysis used for the Robinson property can also be used by other homesellers. The Cobbs, for example, with a $100,000 property should emphasize VA financing. FHA mortgages should be highlighted, providing the local FHA loan limit reaches $100,000.

If the Cobb home is an entry-level property in their community, then deals with little money down (FHA) or no money down (VA) should be promoted. They should stress tax benefits, including the ability to write

Who Can Buy the Robinson House?	
Purchase Price	$240,000
Likely Down Payment	$60,000
Probable Loan Amount	$180,000
Interest Rate	8.5 Percent
Monthly Mortgage Cost	$1,384.04
Monthly Property Taxes	$200
Monthly Insurance	$40
PITI	$1,624.04
Conventional, Fixed-Rate Loan	
Front Ratio, 28 Percent	
Required Monthly Income	$5,800
Required Annual Income	$69,600
Liberal ARM	
Teaser Rate	5.5 Percent
Initial Monthly Payment	$1,022.02
Qualifying Interest Rate	7.5 Percent
Qualifying Monthly Payment	$1,258.59
Monthly Property Taxes	$200
Monthly Insurance	$40
PITI	$1,498.59
Front Ratio, 33 Percent	
Required Monthly Income	$4,541.18
Required Annual Income	$54,494.18

off more than the standardized deduction. The Cobbs should emphasize the joy of going from rental status to ownership ("Why rent when you can buy this charming. . . ").

What you are selling is not just bricks and mortar. You are marketing a lifestyle, an opportunity, betterment, status, ego satisfaction ("You'll be proud to show your friends. . . "), and tax benefits. In a word: values.

WHERE TO MARKET

Once a sales pitch for your property has been developed, the next question is how to get the word out.

The experience of the brokerage community is clear: speak to everyone you know or can reach, even people with no possible interest in your property. Why? Because nonbuyers may have friends, relatives, or co-workers who want a home just like yours.

The first rule of real estate marketing comes directly from the medical profession: do no harm. Whatever you say or write should be positive, a concept that seems fairly obvious until one browses the classifieds.

Real estate classified sections in local newspapers are a proven, effective marketing tool for owners, the very reason such sections are packed with ads. The classifieds give people the opportunity to pick those properties that seem most interesting in privacy and without sales pressure.

But the effectiveness of classified ads is often diminished by messages that devalue the seller's marketing position, such as these examples:

Handyman Special. A home in miserable condition and therefore a property that can be had for less than the asking price.

Price Reduced $12,000. In other words, we couldn't sell it before, so we'll try again at a lower price. A buyer reading such words may well believe that additional discounts are possible.

Just Listed. This expression has value in a hot market, but when times are tough, "just listed" means buyers can wait a few weeks, or months. Without an immediate sale, the owner is likely to accept more pliable terms and prices.

Owner Anxious. Here's a wonderful expression. Can't you just see the owner pacing back and forth, praying for a buyer? Buyers can see such pacing, and when they do they can also see lower prices and better terms.

The list could go on, but the point is that owners and brokers must write ads that project positive images. Here's how an ad should be developed.

Grabber. You need an expression up front that makes your home stand out. A leading industry magazine for brokers and agents, *The Real Estate Professional* (Suite 5, 1492 Highland Avenue, Needham, MA 02192), publishes model newspaper ads in each issue, including some with excellent leads.

- Enjoy the Best—You've Earned It
- Starting Out?
- Peaceful Elegance
- Abundant Living, Bargain Price
- Expect to Be Impressed
- See Worthy

- Financing's a Breeze
- Fireplace Aglow
- A Purse Pleaser
- Postcard Setting
- Your Budget's Best Friend
- Not All Treasure Is Buried
- Buy Today, Reap Tomorrow
- Unrent Yourself
- Turn Your Dollars into Better Quarters
- Head for Our Hills
- No Misprint!

Not one headline or lead above talks about bedrooms, baths, or reduced prices. Each is inviting and engaging, and each will cause buyers to read further.

Location. The ad must specify where the property is located so that buyers looking elsewhere will not waste their time—or yours.

Construction. Is it brick, frame, CBS (concrete, brick, and stucco), adobe, etc.?

Style. Is the property a colonial, split-level, rambler, townhouse, ranch house, Williamsburg, etc.?

Bedrooms. How many bedrooms are available? A bedroom should be private and have at least one window and one closet.

Kitchen. In the world of real estate marketing no home has a plain and simple kitchen. Instead, kitchens are described as galley kitchens, country kitchens, eat-in kitchens, modern kitchens, gourmet kitchens, etc.

Baths. A room with a sink, toilet, and shower stall or bathtub is a "full" bathroom. A room with a sink and toilet is a "half-bath." A room with just a toilet is a "quarter-bath." An outhouse, as some anonymous wit once remarked, can be described as a "bathroom outstanding in its field."

Basements and Attics. If a home has a usable basement or attic, or both, then sellers should say so. The reasoning is that such areas markedly increase the floor space and utility of a home. A rambler, for example, with a full, dry, usable basement has 100 percent more room than a rambler without a basement.

Special Features. All homes have something that makes them desirable, and such features should be mentioned. Good choices include storm windows and doors, trees, flat lots, fenced backyards, a pool, attached garage, central air conditioning, nearby special facilities, etc.

Price. An ad without a price may bring in many phone calls, but such calls are likely to include a large number from people who cannot possibly afford your property. Save time, save energy, and show a list price.

Open House. If the property will be open, give the date (Sunday), hours (1–5), and directions.

Contact . Always include a name and phone number so people can follow up.

Status. Brokers must identify themselves when placing ads; self-sellers need not. If, as a self-seller, you want brokers to call, write "Brokers Invited." If you do not want brokers to participate, write "No Brokers Please."

Given all the items above, how will our ad read? Here's a model to consider.

Classic Living
Fernville: Charm and grace mark this brick colonial with 4 Bd, 3 Ba, huge country kitchen, and full basement. Level, treed lot with fence, 2-car garage. Near public stables, easy access downtown. $235,000. Open Sunday, 1–5. R on Smith, L on Barksdale, L on Plano to 1123. Lem Ford, Zirlig Realty. 555-3500 (O), 555-4754 (H).

WORDS THAT CAN MEAN TROUBLE

Real estate ads have always reflected social values, and when those values discriminate, there is little doubt that people are hurt.

For homesellers, bias is not an idle matter. If you or your broker discriminates—if even a subagent you have never met discriminates—*you* could face serious penalties, perhaps fines and legal costs well into six figures.

The issue is not whether a given homeseller has certain preferences or dislikes, but whether those values enter the stream of commerce. Simply put, once a home is publicly available for sale, it must be equally available to everyone.

Consider what would happen if biased marketing were allowed. The first victims, obviously, would be those denied access to a property. But there is a second group that is hurt, as well: sellers not bright enough to understand how discrimination limits their marketing efforts or the salability of their homes.

Suppose that a town has 2,000 potential buyers for homes priced at $135,000. Suppose as well that 400 of those buyers are left-handed. If Madigan will only sell to a righty, then his pool of buyers is down to 1,600 people. In effect, he has fewer chances to sell his home, there are fewer people to compete for his property (and thus push up the price), and with fewer people his home is more likely to linger on the market.

We have gotten past the point where ads are openly discriminatory ("No blacks allowed"), but there is no shortage of ads that reflect bias of one sort or another.

"Great home in Forest Lakes area, perfect for a young family." This ad suggests that Forest Lakes is less than perfect for single people, those who are not married, and those without children.

"Terrific home for a fine Christian family." The language here is offensive on the basis of religious preference and familial status.

"Hey dudes, here's a swinging bachelor pad not far from the beaches and beauties." Families need not apply, or women, apparently.

"This classic home with six bedrooms is ideal for larger families." What about an individual who wants a lot of space for a model train collection?

Always review ads and marketing materials to assure that information about your property contains no reference to race, religion, creed, national origin, marital status, mental or physical disability, or sexual preference. Such factors, and similar considerations, have nothing to do with a home sale, purchase, rental, or exchange.

Make certain you describe property and not people. Avoid the following words:

1) Adult, mature, empty nester, or senior citizen. (Note: It may be acceptable to use "adult" when discussing properties intended for those aged 55 and older providing such properties are organized within the meaning of the Fair Housing Act. See a real estate attorney for details.)

2) Bachelor, single, or married

3) Couple or couples

4) Children (except for senior housing as specifically provided)

5) Family or families (exceptions: use of the term "family room" or "in-law suite")

6) Christian, Jewish, Muslim, Hindu, etc.

7) Young or old

8) Black, Indian, Negro, white, etc.

9) Foreign or foreigner

10) Straight or gay

Be clear, as well, with the agents you retain. Your home is for sale to anyone who wants it and has the means to buy it. Period. If there is any question or confusion on this matter, avoid problems before they arise and get another agent.

ALTERNATIVE ADVERTISING

When we think of real estate advertising, we usually envision classified ads or display ads placed by builders. There are other ways to get the message out, including some that are cheap or even free.

Most metro areas now support one or more real estate picture guides. Such guides typically accept ads only from real estate brokers, a restriction that gives brokers a marketplace advantage.

Picture guides are usually distributed without cost, published on newsprint, and distributed through local stores and vending machines. They should be regarded as effective, especially thicker books with a large variety of properties.

While picture guides have traditionally been off-limits to self-sellers—and even off-limits to licensed real estate brokers who did not belong to given professional groups—times are changing.

Some picture books or tabloid-style giveaways are now published by organizations that cater specifically to self-sellers. Such publications may be nothing other than an advertising vehicle, while others are part of a marketing package put together by individual brokerage firms for their clients.

Small newspapers—and sometimes larger ones—often publish a "home of the week" story, a feature that commonly includes a photo, pricing information, and a broker's phone number. If your home is interesting in terms of architecture, history, or location, it may be possible to gain coverage for your property. For more information, call your local real estate editor and ask how properties are selected.

If your property is located anywhere near a government facility, university, major company, or hospital, call and ask to speak with someone in the housing office. If there is a housing office, then there will also be a way to list homes for sale or rent, typically without charge. You may be allowed to list a property in a computer file or on a bulletin board.

In the case of military bases, there is commonly a housing office to assist military personnel who require off-base housing. In areas where there are several large military facilities, bases may share housing information—even when facilities for different services are involved. In the Washington, D.C., area, for example, local bases share housing information and anyone willing to lease or sell to active-duty personnel is welcome to use the system. Local real estate brokers make constant use of the military listing service, but the service is open to both brokers and nonbrokers alike.

Around the country there are roughly 1,500 multiple listing services (MLS), and of these, about 1,400 are affiliated with local real estate groups. Seen another way, about 100 MLS systems are not affiliated with the brokerage community and many are open to the public.

Perhaps the largest MLS available to both brokers and non-brokers nationwide is the one found on America Online (AOL), a vast electronic bulletin board with hundreds of thousands of members. AOL members may use the MLS to buy, sell, rent, or exchange property, and they may do so without additional cost or fees other than online charges.

Located in AOL's real estate area (key word: MLS), the system lists everything from apartment flats in Moscow to plush California estates. For more information, call AOL at (800) 827-6364. *Be certain to mention extension 5764 to obtain the free software and online time available at this writing.*

Readers—as a matter of full disclosure—should be aware that the author developed the AOL real estate area and serves as its host. Questions for the author may be left on the real estate area bulletin board, "Ask Our Broker." Real estate software and articles may be downloaded from various libraries in the area, and mortgage rates are posted daily by major national lenders. In addition to the real estate area, at this time America Online features dozens of services and forums, allows members to connect with the Internet system, permits unlimited e-mail, and has more than 50,000 program files online and available for downloading without additional charge other than online connect fees.

There is another marketing choice, but as a practical matter this option is limited to real estate brokers.

Many successful brokers maintain extensive mailing lists. It's not uncommon for top brokers and agents to send out several thousand pieces of mail each month. In fact, one agent—who has listed and sold property worth more than $40 million in a single year—sends out as many as 80,000 pieces of mail a month! Even if only one-tenth of 1 percent of his mailings result in a listing or sale, he will handle 80 transactions a month—potentially business worth several million dollars.

The mega-agent with the big mailing list has the right idea. Reach enough people and somebody, somewhere, will want to buy.

FACT SHEETS

Earlier it had been suggested that sellers should visit open houses to check out the competition, consider prices, and meet brokers. If you visited enough homes you may have reached a point where the property on 12th Street and the home on Vincent Place begin to look alike.

Fortunately there is a cheap and easy cure for the blending problem, one that sells houses.

Every home, no matter how modest, can benefit from a fact sheet, a single page that describes the property and the deal you want.

In an age when a home computer can easily generate attractive and professional-looking information, making a fact sheet is a simple mechanical process. Writing a fact sheet, unfortunately, is more complex.

Within all fact sheets is a hidden problem: if they are not properly expressed they can be used as evidence to show that you or your broker misled some poor, woeful buyer. Given this downside potential, sellers should make certain that fact sheets are absolutely accurate and, as well, that they contain appropriate caveats.

A fact sheet should be seen as a marketing device designed to provide information and create a social opening that will allow buyers to gracefully and comfortably get back in touch.

Here's how to do it.

1) If possible, have an exterior picture of your home.

2) List the basics, floor by floor. As an example, the first floor might have a living room, dining room, kitchen, half-bath, and study. The second floor may have a master bedroom, a central bath, and three additional bedrooms. And so forth.

3) Provide dimensions for major rooms. If you provide dimensions, make certain that somewhere on the fact sheet there is a statement that clearly says, "Notice: all measures approximate. Information concerning this property believed reliable but not guaranteed."

4) List the tax bill for the latest year. Do not suggest what taxes may be in the future because a sale situation may cause an assessment to rise or fall.

5) Provide the legal description. This will help brokers and buyers complete an offer form. For example, 128 Halprin Street may be known legally as "Lot 7, in the subdivision known as Wilson's Bend."

6) List the price. Not the "asking price," a phrase that suggests flexibility, but simply the price.

7) The broker's name, address, phone number, and fax number should be listed. If you are a broker or agent selling your own property, or if anyone in your household with an equitable or legal interest in the property is a real estate licensee, your fact sheet should give clear notice, as in: "Notice: Owner Thomas North is a licensed real estate broker."

8) If the property has been entered into an MLS, include the MLS number.

9) Be certain to mention how additional information can be obtained. For example, the bottom of the fact sheet might say, "For additional information, or to schedule an appointment, please call Ron Walker, DeBeau Realty, at 555-3030 (office) or 555-4738 (home)."

The additional information material is very important because it gives buyers a socially acceptable way to call and ask questions without obligation. Experience has shown that in many cases the information sought by purchasers is either on the fact sheet or in an ad, so often the real reason for calling is not so much to gain additional information as to unleash the bargaining process.

SIGNS

Cruise around any neighborhood and there are always lots of real estate signs. Signs come in various shapes and forms, but they all have one job: sell the property.

Brokerage signs should be informative, graphically attractive, and well maintained. An old sign, beaten up by use and weather, does not convey the professionalism brokers should desire and sellers should demand. (Most signs can be given new life—and new appeal—with a little soap and water.)

Condo and Co-op Requirements

The material in this chapter applies generally to single-family, detached homes. However, special rules—and limitations—may apply to those selling condos, co-ops, and private unit development (PUD) properties.

Governing rules may limit open houses to specific times. The use of signs may be banned, limited, allowed only in certain areas, or permitted only during particular times.

In the case of co-ops, sellers should plainly state on all fact sheets and offer forms that all sale offers are made subject to approval by the co-op board, if such approval is required.

To assure that you and your broker are operating within appropriate bounds, watch other sellers and be certain to ask your condo, co-op, and PUD officers for advice before marketing your property.

What Not to Say

In the process of conversing back and forth with a buyer, be careful not to tread in dangerous areas.

If someone asks, "Is everyone in the area white?" just say flatly, "I can't respond to that question." Always talk about property, not people.

If the property has a tainted past—if there was an ax murder or suicide five years ago—you may or may not have to tell buyers. More than 15 states have laws that limit the information sellers and their brokers must reveal when a property is "stigmatized." The catch is that such laws vary from state to state, so if your property has a questionable past, speak to a knowledgeable real estate attorney to determine what must be said—if anything.

In the case of AIDS patients, special rules apply. According to the Department of Housing and Urban Development, sellers and brokers cannot say anything if an owner or resident has AIDS or has died from AIDS. The reason is that those with AIDS are regarded as having a disability, and are therefore a protected class under federal anti-discrimination rules.

If you are a self-seller, be certain to have signs made professionally for use in the front yard. In addition, have professionally made "arrow" signs to direct traffic if you hold an open house. To determine how many arrow signs you need, trace a route to your home from a major intersection. Make certain to get the number of signs you need, as well as a few spares, just in case a sign is lost or stolen.

Do not use cheap signs; they will diminish your marketplace position. Selling starts from the instant someone sees that you have a property for sale, and if that instant is marked with a shoddy sign that exudes anything but competence and professionalism, you can bet buyers will look for an advantage.

A growing number of signs now include little boxes to hold fact sheets, a very good idea—especially when the sheets are protected from the weather. More technically advanced are signs that broadcast radio messages about the property so that those driving by don't even have to exit their cars to obtain basic information.

OPEN HOUSES

A broker should prepare a marketing plan for your property, including a thorough listing of past sales, currently available properties, and a complete listing of marketing initiatives such as advertising placements, lock boxes, broker open houses, signs, fact sheets, use of an MLS, and open houses for the general public.

Open houses are sometimes a matter of contention because owners routinely want more open houses than a broker is willing to offer.

A seller, for instance, may believe that it makes sense to hold open houses every weekend until the property sells. In theory, such a schedule may have value, but in practice overexposure creates a substantial problem.

If the Joiner house is held open every weekend, it will soon become a drag on the market—the one house that is always open, always available, and obviously unsold. This situation suggests to buyers that if they want the Joiner property they can get it any time, and they surely won't have to pay full price.

If it happens that a buyer makes a low-ball offer for the property, and if the Joiners reject it, the odds are good that no further bargaining will occur. Buyers in such situations will feel misled because implied signals from the Joiners ("We're always open, buy today, buy low") have created the wrong impression. The Joiners—and other sellers—will do better if they hold an open house from time to time, say every three to four weeks in an urban or suburban area. With such a schedule the property is available, but the owners do not appear desperate.

An alternative to an open house is to show homes by appointment. This strategy makes particular sense for more expensive homes, to limit access to prequalified buyers, and for reasons of personal safety.

The view here is that to sell something you've got to show people the goods, but some brokers disagree. They feel that open houses are not an effective marketing tool. As a seller, you should ask local brokers how they have fared with open houses. And if it is argued that open houses are not effective in your community, then ask what marketing strategies do work locally.

As a seller, you should hold open houses on a regular basis or have a broker hold the property open for you. And if you find a broker who feels open houses are a waste of time, point out that open houses are a good place for brokers to demonstrate their sales skills for would-be sellers and to meet prospective buyers—if not for your property then perhaps for another.

OPEN-HOUSE PREPARATION

If your home is being shown, whether through an open house or by appointment, there are steps that should be taken to prepare the property.

- Have your home in show condition. Everything should be perfect.
- Put away clothes and dishes; make beds; rake the lawn, trim the bushes; and dust.
- Remove pets. Some would-be buyers have allergies; others don't like various members of the animal kingdom. If you have an exotic animal in the house—something that bites or is poisonous—be certain to take appropriate precautions. At one open house the door opened and a massive dog—something not much smaller than a pony and obviously raised on stupendous quantities of steroids—came bounding through the front entrance. As the dog calmly chewed on a log, the would-be buyers made a hasty retreat to the safety of their waiting car and never did see the inside of the property. It could have been a gem, but who knows?
- Remove valuables from the property, or at least hide them. Visitors to a home should never open drawers, but it does happen.
- Send children away.
- Place ashtrays around the property or designate the house as "smoke free."
- Keep several pads handy to record visitor names.
- Use signs to identify items that are not for sale, such as washers and dryers or dining-room fixtures. Such signs will make the bargaining process easier.

- Clean the street in front of your home—even if you didn't make the mess.
- Have plenty of fact sheets on hand.
- Have fresh flowers around the house.
- Replace low-watt bulbs with higher wattage ones, consistent with recommended usage. The idea is to make rooms look brighter.
- Throw away junk to produce a sense of greater spaciousness. Think about what you will throw away when you move, and then get rid of such items before you have an open house.
- Some brokers recommend starting a fire in the fireplace or making cookies before buyers arrive.

SHOWTIME

Holding an open house is somewhat like a Broadway opening. Magic is in the air, all is ready, and now all we need are customers to make the day complete.

If your broker is showing the property, leave. Give the broker and prospects the psychological space needed to build a comfortable relationship.

If you're holding your own open house, be prepared to meet three groups of people: explorers, brokers, and buyers.

Explorers want to see your home even though they're not buying. They may have a friend in the market, they're your neighbors, they're nosy, they want to check your color patterns and design sense, they're about to sell and want to see how your home matches up, or they're bored and have decided to entertain themselves by visiting your open house.

It may seem that explorers, as a group, are largely a waste of time, but in fact they have great value to sellers.

Explorers can tell other people about your property. In other words, they can help you spread the word, so always be nice to them.

Explorers also have value in that they will ask many questions and you will have an opportunity to hone your answers and practice your home-showing skills.

We know that buying a home will bring major changes to a buyer, and big change means trauma to most people. The result is that your job is to introduce the property as calmly as possible, working hard not to stir all the nervous juices that lie just below the surface.

The process starts with the greeting ritual. Meet people at the front door, welcome them, and then engineer a trade: "If you'll sign my register, I'll get you a brochure."

To make this work, you should have a registration pad and pen located at or near the front entrance, and you should have brochures located elsewhere. On the pad, or a form made by computer if you prefer, have the date and space for a name, address, and phone number.

Brokers want registration information because in real estate the path to a commission begins when they have "introduced" someone to a property. Having a signed and dated registration sheet is exceptional evidence showing exactly when first contact was made with a prospect. In addition, having names and numbers allows brokers to follow up with prospects, either for your home or for someone else's.

For self-sellers, the value of a registration sheet is somewhat different. You want a registration sheet so that you, too, can follow up with prospects. A few days after an open house, for example, you might want to call prospects and ask if they would like to see the property at their convenience. Offering to show the house again is less aggressive than calling and asking if someone wants to buy.

Registration sheets can also have value if you decide to list your home with a broker. The registration sheets show that you introduced the property to given people, and so you and a broker might amend a listing agreement to account for your work as a self-seller. For example, it might be agreed that you will list exclusively with broker Talbert, but if the home is bought by a prospect you "introduced" to the property, then the commission will be 3 percent of the sale price rather than 6 percent. In effect, you can create a listing that is exclusive only with regard to those individuals brought to the property through broker Talbert.

Once registered and armed with a brochure, offer to answer any questions and then allow explorers to wander the property at their leisure without a broker or owner shadowing their every move. This way they will have the psychic space required to make comments and talk among themselves.

Your home is more than bricks and mortar; it has enormous importance to you in terms of ego and other values, thus there is the temptation to rip out someone's throat should they criticize your flawless decor. Forget it. Different people have different tastes and preferences, and your job as a seller is to do whatever it takes to convert one lucky person to buyer status. If visitors make rude comments at your open house, remember your goal is to sell the property, not debate fashion trends or make friends.

To brokers, your home is a business opportunity and their reason to visit an open house is to determine how they can make money from your transaction. From your perspective, having brokers make money can be very much to your advantage.

If your home is being held open by a broker, then other brokers will visit the property to see how it compares with listings they have, other properties now on the market, and properties they may list in the near future. They will also want to confirm baseline issues such as agency (Is the visiting broker acting as a subagent of the seller, a buyer broker, or a principal buying for his or her own account?) and compensation (Will the listing broker cooperate? If so, under what terms and conditions?).

If you are a self-seller, then brokers will visit to check out the property, introduce themselves, and see on what basis, if any, it is possible to list your property.

For self-sellers, such visits represent a moment of truth. Many Fizzbos, as a matter of purity to the cause of self-selling, refuse to deal with brokers. This may feel good but it can produce a woeful business decision.

Ask yourself a question: why are you selling? If the answer is to get the best possible price and terms for your property—the greatest net benefit—then you're on the right track. If a broker can lead you to the promised land of big bucks and a solid sale, at least listen.

Over the years brokers have become increasingly sophisticated in dealing with self-sellers. Rather than bludgeon Fizzbos with fast talk and loose promises, many have come to understand that the way to win the hearts and minds of self-sellers is to be helpful.

The logic used by brokers goes like this. Whether you sell or not, the broker is a local entrepreneur who relies on a positive public image to gain business. Abusing Fizzbos means that you will share your experiences with neighbors, and that does brokers little good. Thus, as a matter of common sense and good public relations, it is simply good business to treat Fizzbos with respect.

There is another fact that brokers keep in mind when talking with self-sellers: a large number of Fizzbos ultimately use professional services.

A 1991 study by the National Association of Realtors shows that 15 percent of all homes are pure Fizzbo deals. Another 8 percent tried to sell without a broker but ultimately wound up using a professional. In other words, of those who start out as Fizzbos, 35 percent ultimately turn to a broker.

LEVERAGE

As a self-seller you have enormous leverage with brokers if only because you always have the option to just say no. No listings. No cooperation. No nothing.

Then again, would you say yes if the deal were right? As a Fizzbo you can use your leverage to create two important accommodations.

First, while brokers would universally prefer to list homes with exclusive-right-to-sell agreements, you're a self-seller. You can sell by yourself, list exclusively with a broker, list with a broker on something other than an exclusive basis, or hire a broker as a consultant.

Broker Wilton might say, "Well, I have a party in mind who might be interested in your property, but state law says I need a written listing agreement to show a property."

Broker Wilton is right. He needs a written listing. But state law does not say he needs an exclusive arrangement, so if you're interested, a sound response might work like this:

"I've had a number of brokers and agents who want to list the property. I know you can't me tell the name of your prospect, but can you give me some background so I can decide whether or not to go further? For instance, what is their household income, what are their occupations, and why do they want to live in this area?"

If the broker comes back with specifics—they make $62,000 a year, work at a machine shop, and your location would make commuting much easier—then there may well be a buyer. If the broker has no specifics, forget it.

With specifics you can make your first accommodation and agree to list the property. But rather than an exclusive agreement, you can use a 30-day general (open) listing that will allow the broker to show the property as you continue your independent marketing efforts. Since Wilton's goal was to obtain a written listing to show the house to a particular set of buyers, he should be happy.

The second accommodation relates to the not-so-delicate issue of commissions.

Broker Wilton will see his buyers as a potential asset. If he sells them a house, he will get a commission, so from his perspective it makes sense to sell the property that yields the greatest possible commission. As a seller you have a different view.

Whatever you pay to Wilton, or to anyone else, means less money for you at closing. Your goal is thus to have Wilton bring his buyers to the property without paying an excess commission.

As a Fizzbo, it surely makes sense to say to Wilton, "Look, if another broker had listed this property you would have no hesitation about bringing in your prospects. And if the property sold, you would be delighted to receive a co-op commission. Right?

"So, let's say as a practical matter that I've listed the property and I'll pay you a co-op fee, say 3 percent of the sales price. If that works for you, it works for me."

Wilton may or may not accept your offer, but if he does accept and his buyers wind up purchasing from you, then you may cut your brokerage costs in half. That's not a bad deal.

Will Wilton accept? That depends on several factors. If the market is strong, he's likely to accept because buyers are easy to find and your property is just a quick deal. If the market is weak, Wilton will see—or should see—that his buyers have great value. In this case, Wilton is likely to argue for something more than a co-op fee.

Should you pay more than a co-op fee? Your goal is to sell the house for the greatest possible net benefit, but if it doesn't sell for months on end you're paying mortgage bills and taxes that diminish your profits.

You have no obligation to list with Wilton, and in a strong market the very same factors that make buyers so common for him also make them common for you. In a down market, however, a broker with prospects is not to be ignored.

A *word of caution*: Read—or have your attorney read—all listings before signing. Make certain that the listing says what you want it to say, and that it is not an exclusive arrangement or a deal that requires you to pay more than you expect.

BUYERS

Our open house has produced, so far, explorers and brokers. They are surely wonderful people, but in our marketplace hierarchy they are not bearing checks and are therefore of minimal interest.

The folks most certain to catch our attention are buyers, people who are ready to buy, willing to buy, able to buy, and wanting to buy what we've got.

Buyers, unfortunately, do not wear signs or come emblazoned with a large "B" on their foreheads. This is a notable and unfair omission, which means we have to root out such people on the basis of conversation and observation.

What makes a buyer? Think of your experiences when you bought. Home buying is a hostile, discomforting experience filled with financial danger, personal conflict, mounds of paperwork, and lots of people making money from your simple desire to buy indoor living space.

Buyers—when they see a home in which they are seriously interested—are somber folks with serious questions.

> How old is the furnace?
> How long does it take to commute downtown?
> Do the local schools offer special programs for my children?
> How much were taxes last year?

As a seller, it's your job (or your broker's) to answer all questions fairly, openly, and honestly. If something isn't perfect, say so. If you don't have an answer, offer to find out.

The important point is to keep the lines of communication open. Work with your buyers to show how they can overcome problems, or at least make compromises. Listen to their questions, and try to understand their needs.

As you listen to the buyers, ask how you can accommodate their needs while fulfilling your own. What steps can you take to make their decision easier, smoother, and happier?

From conversations between buyers and sellers, or buyers and brokers, most terms of a deal are generally known before the first offer form is unveiled. But buried in that form is the essence of every sale, the details that can create benefits worth thousands of dollars.

12
Selling in a Down Market

For many years, real estate values in most markets have risen faster than the rate of inflation, an economic fact of life that meant home buying represented little risk. If you didn't like the place—if you had to move or wanted to move—all you had to do was sell. And since homes were in demand and prices were rising, real estate sold.

Now the certainty that once ruled the marketplace has crumbled. We know that prices can go up *and* down, and that real estate—like stocks and bonds—is not immune from economic swings.

There is little doubt that some sellers will be forced to enter the marketplace at exactly the wrong time, the moment when sales are slow and prices are steady or falling. What to do?

A careful look at down markets will show that not everyone gets hurt. This is not to say that down markets should be greeted with spasms of joy, but rather that not all sellers will suffer a terrible fate.

Seller Crenshaw, for example, bought his home in 1980 for $39,000 and could have sold two years ago for $230,000. Now his home will only sell for $195,000. To Crenshaw there is a "loss" of $35,000. Crenshaw didn't sell at the top of the market, but what has he lost? True, he has less ability to borrow because the value of his assets has gone down. But look at his checkbook—is any money missing?

Crenshaw is like the investor who moans because he failed to buy a stock at $4 a share and it's now at $91. Sure, it would have been nice, but with the same logic one could complain about buying a lottery ticket that didn't win.

The choices for Crenshaw are not particularly harsh. He can stay where he is. He can refinance because he has plenty of equity. He can sell and pocket a substantial cash profit. He can rent. Because his mortgage is so small, the overwhelming probability is that Crenshaw's property will generate an ongoing monthly income. (Crenshaw must watch the calendar if he rents, however, because if he does not buy a home of equal or greater value within two years he is likely to lose the ability to defer taxes on profits from the sale.)

A more serious problem confronts Dawkins. He bought three years ago at $345,000 with 90 percent financing. His original mortgage was $310,500 but now the property is worth $295,000.

Dawkins is in trouble for two reasons.

First, the down payment—his $34,500 investment in the property—is gone.

Second, Dawkins owes more than the property is worth. To borrow an expression from the auto industry, Dawkins is an "upside-down" owner.

Unfortunately, mortgage balances and home values do not reveal the full extent of Dawkins's problems. Let's say his current mortgage balance is now $308,000. Let's also say that Dawkins can market his home for $295,000. To sell he needs at least $13,000 in cash to pay off the loan.

But there's more. A sale at $295,000 shows the gross amount Dawkins expects to receive. What if he has to pay a point for the borrower, say $2,500. What if a broker is involved in the sale and charges a 6 percent fee? That's $17,700. Suppose that to unload the place Dawkins must pay $2,000 to fix the heating system?

Now—instead of a $13,000 loss, Dawkins is looking at big money, at least $35,200 in cash to get out of the deal, plus another $34,500 in lost equity, for a total of $69,700.

To make matters worse, Uncle Sam has no interest in Dawkins's loss. If Dawkins makes a profit, then Uncle Sam wants to tax it, but if a seller has a loss there is no write-off or tax credit to offset the damage.

For Dawkins the best solution is not to sell. By not selling he has no need to pay $13,000 to the lender, marketing costs, or seller concessions.

Not selling means that Dawkins stays in the property or rents. Job opportunities elsewhere will be lost, he won't be able to get a home-equity loan (because he has no equity), and the personal preference to live elsewhere must go on hold.

As to renting, it's unlikely to be a wonderful solution for Dawkins.

Dawkins has a large mortgage, which means he has high monthly payments. He is renting in a down market, so many homes are likely to be available for lease, a factor that will push down rents. If he hires a broker to manage the property because he moves out of town, Dawkins will have to pay a management fee and—like Crenshaw—if Dawkins rents he must watch the calendar for tax purposes.

Because relatively few people buy property and sell within a short span, marginal falls in real estate prices have little impact on most owners. For those like Dawkins—people who must sell in a down market shortly after acquiring a home—the results can be deadly.

But what if an owner in a down market doesn't want to stay and doesn't want to rent? Can the property be sold?

In an absolute sense, yes, property can be sold with a low price and big concessions. Whether an owner wants to accept such terms is a different question.

The real issue is how to sell in a down market and maximize values. *Recognizing that there is no perfect or ideal solution*, here are several options that may ease matters.

Go for the Gold. Hot markets mean buyers will take anything; slow markets mean the opposite. To succeed, your home must be the best in the community, a property in absolutely wonderful condition that outshines the competition. To sell in a down market means investing in your own home by fixing up and repairing to the extent allowed by finances and sanity.

Change the Broker's Deal. Most homes are sold through the brokerage system, so it follows that if a property is made more interesting to brokers it will have a better chance of selling. If commissions in your community are commonly 6 percent, go to 7 or 8 percent—brokers will respond.

The alternative is to allow a home to linger on the market for months at a time. Suppose the Grady home is on the market for $230,000 and has a $1,600 per month mortgage. Suppose as well that Grady must move in 60 days. For each month past the first two that the property is unsold, Grady loses $1,600 a month, perhaps for many months. By raising the commission from 6 percent to 7 percent, his cost is $2,300. Simply stated, it's a lot cheaper and easier to raise the commission than to agonize for months on end as the property remains unsold.

Take Back Financing. Rather than getting equity out in the form of cash, take back a loan. For example, Higgins has a home valued at $150,000. Drabeck can put down $10,000, and the property has a freely assumable loan of $100,000. To make this deal work, another $40,000 is needed, money that can come from the seller in the form of a $40,000 owner take-back. This approach will raise your monthly income, but it will not provide cash—something you may need to buy the next home.

Pay the Buyer. This may seem like a strange concept since buyers are usually the ones who do the paying, but consider this: lenders allow "seller contributions" to make a deal work. Depending on the lender, the amount down, and the type of loan, "seller contributions" equal to 3 to 9 percent of the sale price may be allowed.

Why give money to your buyer? Because seller contributions may be the only way to move the house in a down market.

For example, if the property is selling for $200,000 you may be able to give the buyer a $6,000 credit toward closing costs. That might be enough to cover all settlement costs for the buyer, meaning that the house can be acquired for the down payment. If the deal is worked correctly, it is possible for *both* buyer and seller to leave closing with checks.

One important advantage of the pay-the-buyer strategy is that it can allow you to change your marketing effort in a way that may be better than a simple price reduction.

For example, if you have a home that's selling for $175,000 but hasn't attracted much interest, you might want to consider a price reduction, say 5 percent less or a new asking price of $166,250. Alternatively, the home may be more appealing to purchasers if you instead offer to pay the first $8,500 in buyer closing costs. "Collect $8,500 at closing" might be a great way to start an ad.

To see if seller contributions make sense, make the deal contingent on a review to be received by you within seven days (or whatever) by the buyer's lender stating that the terms of the agreement are acceptable.

Go to a Lease Option. With this choice, you rent the property and a portion of the rent is credited to the tenant if he or she elects to buy. With a lease option one often finds:

- A premium rental because part of the rent is potentially a cost to the owner if there is a sale.
- A complete rental agreement.
- A sale price known in advance.

How much of the rental is used as a credit, and the sale price, are nego-

tiable items. But lurking beneath the surface of a lease-option arrangement are several other factors.

1) With a lease option, money comes in each month—premium
money that may be enough to cover costs even with a high mortgage.

2) A lease option buys time. Maybe the market will turn around in a
year or two. (Once again, for tax purposes be certain to watch the calendar.)

3) If prices rise above the lease-option value, the tenant will have a
great interest in buying the property—which is what you want.

4) If prices fall or remain below the option price, the tenant may not
want to buy. Even if there is no purchase, at least you've received a premium rent.

5) If the deal is handled by a broker, expect to pay a sales commission and fees to lease the property. If the broker handles the property
while you are out of town, then expect to pay a management fee as well.

What are the negatives in a lease option? Maybe the sale price is not as
high as you might want, perhaps too much of the lease can be a credit to
the buyer, or the tenants may damage the property and not buy, in which
case you'll need to refurbish the place.

Another negative has to do with money. *If the property is financed, it's
possible that a lease-option deal could trigger a loan's due-on-sale clause.*
This is a substantial, serious matter—one reason a lease-option deal should
be thoroughly reviewed by an attorney before this approach is considered.

It's not clear whether a due-on-sale clause will be invoked the moment
a lease option is made. In the usual case a due-on-sale clause only comes
into play when title is transferred, but with a lease-option arrangement
there may never be a transfer. If ownership changes, then there is no
question as to the right of a lender to enforce a due-on-sale clause.

Conversely, some lenders say that by its nature, a lease-option agreement shows an intent to sell within the meaning of a due-on-sale clause,
and therefore they have a right to call the loan.

Lower the Price. Not a solution for short-term owners, but those who
have held property for a longer period may well be forced to accept a
lower price. The alternative may be months or years on the market, time
that means ongoing mortgage payments, taxes, and other costs to maintain the property.

If you lower your price, lower with care. An ad that blares "Price
Reduced $25,000" says the seller has a very unrealistic view of the mar-
ketplace or is desperate—conditions for buyers to exploit.

Beware of No-Money-Downers. No matter how tempting, avoid folks who want to "save your credit" and "prevent your foreclosure" by purchasing your home with no money down. If their intentions are so noble, then surely they can pay market value rather than 20 or 25 percent off. And certainly they want you to have cash from closing so you can buy your next home.

Deals with no money down mean that *buyers have no risk*. You're not getting cash for your property, the buyer has no equity (and perhaps no job or credit, either), and they must either live in the property or rent it out. If the property is used as a residence then monthly costs are as high as they can be because the entire deal is financed. If they want to rent, in a down market they will have huge problems generating the rentals required to underwrite the deal because many homes will be available for lease.

Strategies used by no-money-downers can be very troublesome. For instance, a buyer may offer to purchase your home with a $20,000 bond instead of cash. But how good is the bond? How much will it sell for *today*? If it can be sold today, why doesn't the buyer sell it? If it is a zero-coupon bond, then it has been bought at a discount today and will only reach its face value in ten or fifteen years. And what if the party issuing the bond defaults? It does happen.

Other ideas from no-money-downers include trades for cars, "jewelry," "art," and "antiques." Can you sell such items for their estimated market value? Can the no-money-downer?

Good luck.

Become a Landlord. Renting the property has the advantage of monthly cash flow to offset carrying costs, but there is another set of advantages that should not be overlooked.

If you sell a personal residence at a loss, the government does not provide any credit or deduction to compensate for your misfortune, a sorry contrast to Uncle Sam's position when you have a profit.

But if you rent the property, and if you intend to make a profit, charge fair-market rentals, and do everything you can to create an economic winner, you no longer have a personal residence. You have an investment, and if you sell an investment at a loss the money you lose is generally deductible. In addition, you can write off repair costs, management fees, condo charges, etc.

As the owner of investment property you will lose the right to take a one-time deduction of $125,000 if you are age 55 or older, and you will lose the right to defer taxes on your profit if you buy a new prime residence of equal or greater value. But if you have a loss, what's the value of such provisions anyway?

Given the alternatives, if renting seems attractive, speak with a knowledgeable tax attorney, CPA, or enrolled agent before taking any action to assure that what you are doing is correct, proper, and appropriately documented.

Try an Auction. Traditionally reserved for tax sales and foreclosures, auctions have found new life as an alternative to orthodox marketing plans, especially when markets are slow.

The great attraction of an auction is that it creates a hyped-up, emotional atmosphere where bidding may not be related to reality. While it is possible to get an auction bargain, it is also possible to pay retail or even higher. As a seller, you should be so lucky as to have a bidding frenzy that produces a sky-high price.

The auction process begins with the retention of a real estate broker qualified to conduct an auction, or an auctioneer licensed in your state who deals with real estate and not just jewelry or antiques. Ask how the auctioneer has sold properties such as yours, why properties have not sold (if that is the case), the fees involved in selling, and the costs you will face if the property is auctioned but does not sell.

Your auction will differ from a foreclosure or tax sale for several reasons, all of which make your property attractive. Your home is occupied rather than abandoned, title is unquestionably clear and marketable, and the property will be in show condition (just as if it were held open by you or a broker). Moreover, buyers need not worry about evicting current owners or squatters, problems that sometimes crop up with foreclosed properties, nor is there any fear that the owners can get the property back under a "right of equity redemption."

Prior to the auction, prospective buyers will have an opportunity to review the auction brochure, a document that explains the auction rules and requirements and also provides property information. Buyers will also have a chance to inspect the property for a week or two before the auction. The most sophisticated prospects will tour the home and are likely to bring along real estate brokers (to get an estimate of market value) and a home inspector (to determine the condition of the property).

At the auction itself, only registered bidders will be allowed to bid on the property. To bid, typically, an individual will have to show that enough cash is available to make a down payment on the property, cash that can be in the form of a certified check, cashier's check, or money order payable to the bidder. If a bidder wins, the check or money order is then assigned to the auctioneer and is non-refundable.

Before offering a property, the auctioneer will explain the rules. Properties can be offered at absolute auction so that whoever has the highest bid wins—even if the highest bid is $1. An auction with a reserve price works differently. Here the auctioneer and seller have established a secret minimum market value and announced that the property is being sold subject to a reserve price. If the highest bid exceeds the reserve price, the property is sold. If the highest bid is below the reserve value, then the seller has the right to withdraw the property from the market.

Having won and made a deposit, the bidder usually has 30 to 60 days to finalize the transaction. If the money is not available and the deal can't be closed, the buyer's deposit can be forfeited.

As a seller, you are interested in not only a sale but a sale that results in the highest possible net benefit for you. With an auction you are likely to pay a fee in advance equal to 2 or 3 percent of the projected selling price. If the property sells, there is then an additional fee, say 6 or 7 percent of the final sales price. All prices and costs should be regarded as entirely negotiable.

Look at Contests. While auctions are becoming more frequent, a few sellers are taking a different route: they are converting homes into contest prizes.

If a contest seems somewhat unusual, it is. The basic problem is that setting up a contest without a skill requirement is regarded as a lottery operation in most states, and thus illegal.

But matters may be different in those jurisdictions where non-profit organizations are allowed to conduct lotteries, or in situations where a contest does not depend on chance to produce a winner.

In the case of a non-profit organization, a home may simply be first prize in a lottery or contest. If Corona has a house worth $125,000, then a local charity might make this deal: it will conduct a lottery with the Corona property as first prize. Tickets will be priced at $100 each, so 1,250 tickets will have to be sold before the house can be awarded. Corona will agree to pay $5,000 for advertising, postage, and other costs. If more than 1,250 tickets are sold, all proceeds from the additional tickets will go to the charity. If 1,250 tickets are not sold, at Corona's option either the property will be awarded or all ticket money will be returned.

Can this work? You bet. A rural Virginia estate on 18 acres was marketed through a contest sponsored by a local charity. More than 3,600 tickets were purchased, enough to buy the home and generate a profit for the charity.

An alternative to lotteries is an essay contest, such as those that have occurred in Texas (1981), Washington, D.C. (1986), Pennsylvania (1993), and Maine (1992, 1993). The way it works is that individuals submit essays on an assigned topic and the best essay wins the house. The contest has specific rules, such as a minimum number of entries, standards for judging the entries, the selection of judges (the owner should never act as a judge), and required entry fees. Note that a simple drawing without an essay would depend entirely on luck and therefore would be illegal in most states. It is the use of an essay, the element of skill, that makes essay contests acceptable in some jurisdictions.

Probably the best-known contests have originated in Maine. In one case, a 188-year-old inn was won by a Maryland couple who sent in an entry plus $100. The contest drew more than 7,000 entries. Of this number, 5,000 entries were involved in the contest (thus creating a $500,000 sales price for a property appraised at $525,000), and more than 2,000 were returned to entrants once the sales plateau was reached.

If you have an interest in a lottery or contest, be certain to speak with an attorney first to ensure that what you want to do is entirely legal. Because the use of charitable lotteries and contests to market homes is extremely rare, it may make sense to have a letter from your state attorney general approving your game plan. In addition, check with postal authorities to assure you are not in violation of regulations concerning illegal interstate pyramid schemes or other rules.

FORCED SALES: FORECLOSURE AND BANKRUPTCY

While selling real estate is usually voluntary and profitable, that's not always the case. People have problems. Illnesses, accidents, business failures, divorces, and the death of a spouse can lead to hard times and a need to sell.

In periods when there is a strong local economy, being forced to sell may not be pleasant, but it is plausible. But for those who need to sell when homes are not readily marketed, a tough situation becomes infinitely worse.

Regardless of the reason, if you do not make mortgage payments, lenders will take whatever actions are necessary to protect their loans, including foreclosure. Even if you make up lost payments, the lender may still have the right to foreclose since bringing the mortgage up to date in such instances merely means the lender is owed less, not necessarily that the problem is resolved.

Foreclosure practices vary around the country, but in general terms an auction will be scheduled within a given period and the property will be sold for the greatest possible price.

That the property has been sold at foreclosure does not always mean the owner no longer has any claim to it. There is likely to be an "equitable right of redemption" that allows an owner to recover his or her property by paying all past-due obligations, late fees, legal costs, and other charges within a given period, say as long as a year.

At the auction the lender will typically make a bid for at least the amount of the loan and all legal costs. In effect, for anyone to buy the property they must pay off the lender who holds the first trust or first mortgage. If no one makes an adequate bid, the property is "won" by the lender.

In the auction process, the rights of second-trust holders and others have little protection, especially in a down market. The rule is that all claims by the first-mortgage holder must be paid before a dime is available to the second-trust lender. A bid equal to the first trust will effectively wipe out the second-trust lender—unless he or she wants to bid for the property.

If the auction is a success and raises more money than is owed, you may actually get a check. If it happens that the property sells for less than the amount of the first trust, late fees, and legal costs, lenders in many states will seek a deficiency judgment to collect the money not raised by foreclosure. The catch is that some states, such as California, have what is known as a "single-action" rule, a rule that prohibits lenders from seeking a deficiency judgment after a foreclosure.

It may seem that the lender has a powerful position, and while the lender has enormous leverage you have some bargaining power as well.

Foreclosures can be postponed if an owner declares bankruptcy, a serious matter that should be avoided unless no other alternative is available. *If you cannot make mortgage payments, if foreclosure or bankruptcy seem probable, consult with a bankruptcy attorney immediately.* You can go from homeownership to homelessness very quickly if you do not act to protect your interests.

An attorney can contact lenders and inform them that you would like to work out a reasonable arrangement that involves neither foreclosure nor bankruptcy. Lenders will be interested because they don't want to foreclose (it looks terrible on their records); they don't want to be the high bidder (lenders do not want to own real estate); and bankruptcy rules are strange. For instance, if there was a foreclosure before a bankruptcy and the winning bid was low (whatever "low" might be), a bankruptcy court in some cases can set aside the foreclosure and void the sale.

Another problem for lenders is that a bankruptcy can result in a "cramdown" situation. The court gathers all creditors and hammers out a settlement. Since the lender has no way of knowing what a court will decide, it may be safer to work with the borrower.

The Supreme Court, in *Nobelman et ux v. American Savings Bank* (92-641), decided in 1993 that a mortgage is a contract between a lender and a borrower and that the amount owed to the lender could not be reduced in a Chapter 13 bankruptcy because property values had fallen. At the same time, there are various types of bankruptcies and in a bankruptcy proceeding a lender is a creditor; creditors routinely obtain less than 100 cents on the dollar from bankruptcy courts, so bankruptcy procedures are hardly risk-free for mortgage lenders. (Note: A Chapter 13 bankruptcy allows creditors to work out their debts over a five-year period under court supervision.)

There are a number of non-foreclosure, non-bankruptcy strategies that can be employed when a borrower is in big trouble. None of the following approaches is easy, quick, or cheap, but they may be better than the bankruptcy alternative.

Strategy 1: Refinance. If you do not as yet have late or missed payments, look for a loan with lower monthly cost payments, such as a two-step mortgage, a graduated-payment mortgage, or an ARM. Each of these loans starts off with very low monthly payments, perhaps low enough to make the property affordable. Refinancing may allow you to avoid foreclosure, bankruptcy, or devalued credit.

Strategy 2: Modify. Mortgages are contracts and contracts can be modified by mutual agreement. While a refinancing envisions a new loan and possibly a new lender, a loan modification means taking the mortgage you now have and changing the terms. For example, you may be able to get a lower rate or a longer term, or both. The result will be smaller monthly costs.

Lenders will not modify a loan unless it is in their interest to do so. It is your job to explain—and document—why a modification is necessary and to show how the lender will benefit. Not going to foreclosure and not dealing with a bankruptcy should be seen as benefits in this situation.

Strategy 3: Re-schedule (Forbearance). If the problem you have is temporary—an illness, accident, short-term unemployment, etc.—it may be possible to work out a settlement with the lender that allows unmet mortgage payments and late fees to be added to the mortgage principal or paid out over a given period. In this situation there is no foreclosure or bankruptcy, but your credit report may show several late payments. If re-scheduling is possible, then everyone is ahead, especially in situations where there are a glut of properties on the market and the lender could lose equity by foreclosing.

Strategy 4: Turn in the Keys. Also known as a "deed in lieu of foreclosure," in this situation it is accepted that you cannot make payments, that the property will go to foreclosure, and that your equity is lost. You (or your attorney) contact the lender and ask if they or a buyer would like to acquire the property for the value of the mortgage in exchange for the settlement of all claims. Since a foreclosure is expensive and costly, and since a foreclosure complicated by a bankruptcy proceeding can be excruciatingly long and expensive, a lender might just agree to your proposal.

Some word of caution: If a home is sold by foreclosure, then generally the debt of second-trust holders and others with liens are eliminated. When you turn in the keys to a lender, second trusts and other debts are *not* wiped out. Thus, lenders are unlikely to accept keys to a property when other debts remain outstanding.

A second point is this: If a deed in lieu of foreclosure seems to make sense, meet with an attorney before speaking to a lender. Then—without mentioning your name—have the attorney contact the lender. Your bargaining position is likely to be stronger with professional representation.

Strategy 5: Deal with the Private Mortgage Insurer. If you bought a home with less than 20 percent down and did not use FHA or VA financing, then it's probable that a private mortgage insurer is in the picture.

Because you financed with private mortgage insurance, you were allowed to buy with less than 20 percent down. If you default, the private mortgage insurer will cover the lender's loss up to a certain limit or—in about 30 to 40 percent of all defaulted loans—the insurer will simply acquire the property.

The insurer does not want the property, particularly in a down market. In addition, the insurer does not want to pay out a full claim if the matter can be resolved at a lower cost. That's why it may be possible to work with the insurer.

For example, to avoid a worse situation the insurer may elect to make up your back mortgage payments—but only if the lender agrees not to foreclose.

In this situation you are likely to have credit problems (those late and unpaid monthly bills) and you will certainly owe the insurer for the money it has put up. However, you may gain enough time to get back on your feet or to sell the property without having either a foreclosure or bankruptcy.

Strategy 6: Go to the MAP. If you bought with an FHA loan and run into problems, the Department of Housing and Urban Development (HUD) operates a program known as the "mortgage assignment program" (MAP) that can help.

You can qualify for MAP by reaching several dreadful benchmarks—you've missed a bunch of payments (generally three in a six-month period will do it) and the lender has sent notices of intent to foreclose.

At this point you apply, quickly, to enroll in the MAP program. HUD can then step in and buy the mortgage. Now the lender is HUD and HUD is there to help. The attractions of the HUD program are that you need not sell your home, you can have up to five years to begin loan repayments, and you avoid foreclosure and bankruptcy.

To find out more about the MAP program, contact your lender or area HUD office. Note that when a lender sends out a foreclosure notice for an FHA loan, they must include information about the MAP option.

Strategy 7: The VA Compromise. If you have VA financing and cannot make mortgage payments, the Department of Veterans Affairs (DVA) will take over the loan, much like HUD. VA, however, wants the home on the market and for sale. Once the property is sold, all proceeds up to the loan amount go to DVA. If there's a shortfall, for example, if you owe $80,000 and have $75,000 from the property sale to repay DVA, they'll take the $75,000 and require you to repay the $5,000 balance.

The good news is that DVA will charge a low interest rate to repay the shortfall. The bad news is that until the shortfall is repaid, all DVA benefits are suspended.

Strategy 8: The COW Committee. VA loans made prior to March 1, 1988, may be assumed without a credit check or income qualification. This can be an important sale advantage when the buyer has poor financial qualifications, but there is a hook: if you sell and the buyer defaults, you're liable for the mortgage balance.

Whether this is a serious problem or not will depend on how much was owed and how much equity is in the property. If there is enough value, the sale price can cover the old VA loan and that's the end of the problem.

But if a sale or foreclosure does not repay the loan in full, then you can be required to make up the difference. This is not an idle threat because you can be hit with a deficiency judgment to make up the loss—perhaps thousands of dollars.

Sometimes, though, the letter of the law is too harsh, especially when veterans have acted in good faith. To assist veterans who sold homes with freely assumable loans for which they are still liable, DVA has established a "compromise and waiver" (COW) committee to review such cases. The committee has the ability to reduce or eliminate DVA claims, depending on the facts and circumstances in each case.

For information and forms concerning the COW committee, contact your local DVA office.

Strategy 9: Loss Sharing. A down market hurts everyone and the goal of borrowers, lenders, governmental agencies, and insurers is to come out whole and experience as little damage as possible.

If you face foreclosure and bankruptcy, you have big problems. One defense, oddly enough, is that your problems can be used as a lever to get relief from other parties to the mortgage.

You may have a $175,000 mortgage but a house that is only worth $160,000. After closing, perhaps $145,000 will be left—an amount $30,000 below the mortgage. In some states you can be hit by a deficiency judgment, but a bankruptcy wipes out all debt and will allow you to start clean, so the value of a judgment to a lender is possibly zero.

Lenders don't like zero, so maybe there is a better solution. Perhaps the lender will reduce its claim by $15,000 and allow you to pay $15,000 in the form of a low-interest loan. Is this a good deal for a lender? Will a lender be jubilant? Probably not, but perhaps this approach is less costly and more tolerable than any alternative.

Strategy 10: Sell at a Loss. This is perhaps the hardest choice because it enables an individual to avoid foreclosure and bankruptcy—but at the cost of significant economic hardship.

In this situation you sell the property and have a loss, say $25,000. You must repay the lender and so several options are open.

One choice is to enter into a loan agreement with the lender so that you can pay off the debt over time. A second alternative is to sell family possessions such as cars and furniture to raise the money you need.

A third option is to pull money out of a retirement account. This choice is costly in the long term (less cash for retirement) and costly in the short run as well—it's entirely possible that the money you withdraw will be subject to current income taxes as well as a penalty. Speak to a CPA, tax attorney, or enrolled agent for details.

Strategy 11: State Aid. In selected instances, states may have programs to assist homeowners facing foreclosure. In 1985, Iowa passed debt-moratorium legislation that allowed farmers to delay foreclosure by as much as a year. In Massachusetts, in early 1993, legislation was proposed that would require a court hearing before a foreclosure could be held. In Maryland, a state law provides that when a second trust has a balloon payment, borrowers in certain circumstances can delay postponement of the balloon—and thus foreclosure—for as much as two years.

To see if special programs, rights, or remedies are available in your state, consult with a knowledgeable attorney.

In fact, whether markets are up or down, if you're in financial trouble for any reason, speak to a knowledgeable attorney immediately. Know what your rights are and consider your options. Understand that there are no great and wonderful answers, but it may be possible to avoid foreclosure, escape bankruptcy, and even save your equity and other assets by working with lenders. Understand as well that time counts; you must act quickly to secure as many rights as possible and to protect your position.

Also, be aware that if a lender accepts less than the value of the mortgage in settlement of all claims, then another problem can arise: taxes. The money *not* collected by the lender may be regarded as income by the

IRS and your state. Speak to a tax attorney, CPA, or enrolled agent for complete details.

Another by-product of tough times is likely to be a lousy credit record, something that will make it terribly difficult to buy another home, especially in the short term. For advice regarding credit matters, contact the local office of the National Foundation for Consumer Credit at (800) 388-2227.

13
Looking at Contracts

The very moment a home is first offered for sale, the process of bargaining and negotiation begins, a process that only ends at closing.

How well you bargain is not an idle matter. A real estate deal is a package that includes pricing, terms, and even the kitchen sink. Miss an item here, make an unwitting concession there, and suddenly benefits worth thousands of dollars are gone.

Real estate deals occur within a predictable zone of negotiation. The top of the zone is defined by the price and terms a buyer is willing to pay for the property. The bottom of the zone is bounded by the least attractive price and terms a seller will accept.

The zone of negotiation is not just about prices. A sale package includes both pricing and terms, and the ability to manipulate both is central to successful bargaining.

Take the Tate house. Buyer Evans will not pay more than $145,000 for the property, even though similar homes are selling for $155,000. Should Tate give up? Not at all.

A careful look at other home sales shows that to get $155,000, owners have made a variety of concessions. Most have been willing to pay two points, or roughly $3,000 at closing. All have agreed to replace the old roofs that remain on the twenty-five-year-old houses, an expense of nearly $4,000 per house. Several sellers have agreed to replace old air conditioners, make repairs, paint the first floor, replace washers and dryers, and even repave a driveway—concessions that have typically cost $3,500 per house. In effect, homes that sell for $155,000 have been loaded down with concessions worth $10,500, leaving sellers with a net value of $144,500 before marketing costs and closing expenses.

Looking at the deals made by neighbors, Tate decides that he can actually come out ahead by selling with the right conditions. He agrees to sell to Evans for $145,000, but without an obligation to make repairs, replace the washer and dryer, or pay points. Since the price is so "low," Evans agrees to pay the first $1,000 owed by Tate at settlement.

Now Tate has a deal where he is receiving $145,000 for the house plus a $1,000 credit at closing. That totals $146,000 before marketing costs and closing expenses, $1,500 more than neighbors are receiving.

The deal, as people say, is in the details and those details are found in the world's least glamorous piece of paper, the basic real estate agreement—a formal document typically distinguished by tiny type and convoluted language.

People often look at a real estate sales form and say, "Aha, a contract." In fact, *an unsigned form is not a contract*, it's merely a piece of paper that is entirely worthless without the agreement of a buyer and seller.

In real estate, and in the contracting process in general, to have a contract there must be an offer and there must also be acceptance. If Ross offers $184,000 for a property and Jenkins agrees, we have an offer ($184,000) and an acceptance ("Sure, I'll pay that much").

If Jenkins says "I'll pay $184,000 but you must leave the washer and dryer behind," we have two events. First, the original offer to sell at $184,000 is dead. Second, we have a counter-offer on the table.

Even if we have a written agreement with offer and acceptance, we still need "consideration" to make the deal work. Consideration in a real estate transaction typically means that a buyer will make a deposit with an offer, cash designed to show serious intent and to compensate the owner if the deal falls through under certain circumstances.

(If you sell to a family member or friend, then it's possible to have a deal with "good" consideration—love and affection rather than cold cash.)

The basic real estate forms used locally are likely to cover many issues and in some cases may even be used without alteration. However, as real estate deals have become increasingly complex, more and more deals involve not only basic contract forms but also "addenda"—additions to a contract form made on separate sheets of paper. (Two sheets are "addenda," one sheet is an "addendum.")

Addenda are important because if properly written they supersede contrary or conflicting language found in the basic form. Always have addenda carefully reviewed by a knowledgeable real estate attorney to assure that the meaning of such additions is fully understood.

If someone says their form is the local "standard" and cannot be modified, look out. All forms can be modified by mutual agreement, and all provisions are subject to modification except when established by law.

Real estate agreements can be oral, but generally to be *enforceable* they must be in writing and they must be made by people who are legally competent. The ability of alcoholics, drug users, lunatics, senile individuals, bigamists, and minors—among others—to make contract is questionable at best.

If you list your property with a broker, be certain to first obtain a copy of the offer form used by the broker. Review it carefully with the broker and, if you like, with an attorney. Know what the form says, and understand the obligations it can create.

FORMS

Virtually all jurisdictions have standardized form agreements that are appropriate for local home sales. You must use a local form, rather than a generalized national form, because local jurisdictions commonly require specific items to have a valid real estate agreement. In my community, for example, buyers must be advised of the location of nearby heliports—a clause not found in national forms. And while information related to where helicopters land may seem irrelevant to a real estate deal, a contract without appropriate language in my community may be void or voidable.

We know that to make a deal everything must be in writing, and we know as well that local offer forms are common. The catch is that local offer forms are not designed to create balanced, neutral deals between buyers and sellers.

Historically, the real estate marketing system has been oriented to represent seller interests. One result is that form agreements commonly favor sellers, good news for owners because one can often find a raft of buyer concessions buried in standardized forms.

To see the power of form agreements, imagine that you have found an acceptable selling price and then said to the buyer, "By the way, I want you to pay an extra $2,500 to cover my transfer tax expenses." The buyer would probably question your sanity as well as the marital status of your parents at the time of your birth. But if a form says the buyer will pay all state transfer taxes, the matter only becomes negotiable if the buyer raises the issue. And most buyers, most of the time, won't bargain over items that are part of the standard, usual, normal forms that "everyone" uses. In effect, form agreements "negotiate" a variety of issues by making them seem minor and unimportant.

While most form agreements favor sellers, some do not. Not one contains language that says, "This is a pro-buyer form." *To protect your interests, you must review offer forms carefully, something that should be done with an attorney or broker prior to placing your home on the market.* In the case of an attorney, the cost of such a review is minimal, while brokers will be delighted to examine forms as part of their efforts to sell realty services.

ORAL OFFERS

It is inevitable that someone will see your home, look around, and then start a conversation that goes something like this.

"Look, I see you want $238,000 for this house, and it's a very nice place, but it would be an impossible stretch for us. Would you consider $225,000?"

What we have with such conversation is the start of a downward spiral. If you say, "Yes, $225,000 sounds interesting," then you've immediately lost $13,000 and the buyer isn't even breathing hard.

The buyer never said he (or she) was willing to pay $225,000. He merely asked if you would take such an offer. If you say yes, then a buyer has no reason to go higher than $225,000, and much reason to go lower.

What will happen next, if the buyer is smart, is that he will say, "Let me think about this, perhaps we can come up with an offer everyone can accept."

In the end you may well get a written offer—for $219,000, or $211,999, or whatever. And with terms that will cut your profit by thousands of dollars.

The point is that *as soon as you mention any price other than the listing price, you lose.* As for listing brokers, their agents, and subagents, if they mention any price other than the listing price, they have violated their agency obligations and may be liable for a litany of penalties and damages.

So how do you handle a feeler?

You toss the ball back in the buyer's court.

"Would you take $225,000 for this property?" asks the buyer.

"We have a listing price of $238,000. If you want to make a written offer, we'll certainly review it with care."

"But I don't want to waste your time or mine," says the buyer. "Before going further I need to know if you would consider $225,000."

"We will certainly consider $238,000. If you like the house and want to buy it, then you'll have to provide a written offer. If you're serious, bring us an offer on paper and we will both find out whether or not to continue."

"Well," asks the buyer, "is your price flexible?"

"You mean would we take less than the asking price? That's obviously a question we can't answer without a written offer in front of us."

(The expression "flexible" in real estate largely means that someone will make additional concessions. Thus if a buyer asks, "Is your price flexible?" you can bet that he or she is not asking for the opportunity to pay you more.)

If the bargaining position advocated here seems harsh and unyielding, consider the alternative. As a seller you simply have no reason to make concessions before the formal bargaining process begins.

Ask yourself: what's the point of selling your home? Are you selling to make someone else rich? Or is your goal to get the most money and the best possible terms?

Through the use of seemingly innocent questions, someone may well be asking you to make concessions worth thousands of dollars—perhaps enough to buy a car or send a child to college for a year.

Always answer questions. Always be polite. But never forget your purpose, and never forget that an oral offer is fully worth the paper on which it's printed.

TERMS

If not an oral offer, then you must get something on paper, probably a few pages in the guise of a nicely printed form.

What's in a standardized form? The answer will depend on where you live, but here are the central issues every form agreement should cover.

Price. Item number one for everyone is the matter of price, a specific figure that like a check is usually written in both numerals and words.

Deposits and Damages. A deposit is "consideration," but it is also something more: leverage to assure that the buyer goes through with the deal.

In a deal with a real estate broker, deposit money is placed in an "escrow" or trust account where funds are held apart from the broker's money. Once placed in an escrow account, the money will only be released if both buyer and seller agree. If there is a dispute over the money, the deposit will not be released but instead will be turned over to a court until the matter is settled.

The logic here is that if a broker releases the money without permission of both buyer and seller, he or she may have a liability.

If a deposit is forfeited, then a typical real estate agreement will provide that the money is divided equally between the seller and the broker, at least until the full value of the broker's commission has been paid off. For example, let's say that Hughes offers $100,000 for the Werner house and includes a $15,000 deposit with his offer. Let's also say that broker Rhodes is entitled to a 6 percent commission. If Hughes changes his mind and loses his deposit, the deal is likely to work this way: broker Rhodes would have received $6,000 if the deal went to closing, so he has a $6,000 claim against the deposit. The deposit is $15,000 so it would be divided first with $6,000 to seller Werner and $6,000 to broker Hughes. The remaining $3,000 would go to Werner.

Some form agreements say that by accepting a deposit the seller and broker have no further claims against the buyer. A more liberal arrangement, at least from the seller's viewpoint, allows the seller to take the deposit and still sue the buyer.

A seller can also sue a buyer to induce "specific performance," a phrase that means the buyer will be compelled to go through with the entire deal. As a practical matter, specific performance is rarely obtained in a residential dispute.

If you're a self-seller, it makes sense to place deposit money in your attorney's escrow account, or in an escrow account established with a local bank or savings and loan association.

Because a deposit can be a substantial amount of money, and because closing may not occur for several weeks or months, it's possible to earn interest on an escrow fund. As a seller you should favor receiving all interest, especially if the deposit is forfeited. If a compromise is necessary, agree to split the interest with the buyer, except in the case of default.

If the deal goes through, the deposit will be a credit to the buyer at closing, an amount that can be included as part of, or all of, the down payment.

One question that constantly arises is how much sellers should require for a deposit. The answer is as much as possible—but only within the context of the deal. A big deposit gives you leverage as well as more protection in the event of default. At the same time, demands for a large deposit may scare away buyers.

Location. A form agreement should show the property address (2537 Vine Street) as well as the legal description (Lot 83, Block 21, in the Davis Subdivision located in Cedric County).

At first the matter of location may seem fairly dull because houses, in the usual case, do not move. However, location is an important issue on several levels.

A buyer will want to be certain that the house they like at a given street address is the same piece of ground described in local land records. Thus one reason for a title search.

Assuring that a property is where it's supposed to be is also important because property lines may bend over time. A fence may be a few inches over a property line or a detached garage may actually be located on a neighbor's property, or vice versa.

To prove that buyers are getting all the property described in local land records, and to guarantee as well that the fine-looking gazebo in the backyard is actually on the property, buyers will generally require a survey.

The contract wording may say nothing about a survey, but ultimately a survey will be required. Here's why. If the borrower needs a loan to make the deal work, and a lender requires a survey before agreeing to finance the sale, then there will be a survey—even if the contract says nothing about surveyors.

Financing. A form agreement may provide for an all-cash sale, but as a practical matter such blanks are likely to be labeled "n.a.," or "not applicable."

Most people will need a loan and a sales form will provide space for several important loan features.

First, how much is being borrowed? Take the sale price, subtract the down payment (not the deposit), and the result is the loan amount.

Second, what is the interest rate? Sale forms tend to be tricky on this issue. For example, form language may state that the deal will go through if the buyer can find financing at "7 percent per annum or the minimum prevailing rate at closing." Translated into English, this phrase says that the buyer is now committed to pay whatever interest rate is available when the property goes to closing, language that very much favors seller interests. The 7 percent figure is irrelevant at best, misleading at worst. It simply has no bearing on the deal.

As a seller you do not want a clause that says the buyer is only obligated to go through with the deal if the interest rate is "not more than 7 percent" because if rates rise prior to closing, the sale may die and the buyer will be entitled to a full deposit refund.

Third, the sale papers will stipulate the "loan fees" or points that buyer and seller must make. Here again, look for tricky language.

A point is equal to 1 percent of the amount borrowed, so if a home sells for $200,000 and the buyer pays $20,000 in cash, $180,000 will have to be financed. If you agree to pay one point at closing, you are committed to pay $1,800. If you agree to pay two points, then you must give up $3,600 at closing.

A pro-seller form will simply say that you, the seller, will pay no more than one point or whatever. However, since interest rates and points fluctuate, you want the *buyer's* obligation to be flexible. A good form, for example, might say that the buyer will pay one point as well as any "reasonable" increase or decrease in the number of points required to close the deal. Once the buyer agrees to be flexible, the one point mentioned in the sales form is immaterial.

Fourth, other loan matters will also be spelled out, including:

- The loan term
- The monthly payment for principal and interest
- Whether the debt is a first or second trust
- If the financing is fixed or adjustable
- Whether the loan format is conventional, FHA, or VA
- Whether the loan is technically a mortgage or a deed of trust

(In general terms, a "mortgage" is a loan where the note is held by the lender. A "deed of trust" is an arrangement where a loan is made by a lender, but the note is held by a trustee.)

Fifth, what happens if financing is not available under the terms outlined in the offer? Form agreements routinely provide that the deal is finished, and that the buyer—after a good-faith effort to obtain a loan—is entitled to the return of his or her deposit.

Application. As a seller you want the buyer not only to apply for a loan but to apply instantly. Many forms have a provision requiring a buyer to apply for financing within a given time, say 10 calendar days from the date the contract is signed. If a buyer does not apply for financing within the specified period, the deposit can be forfeited. Application clauses also include language by which the buyer agrees to provide all necessary paperwork and credit information to the lender.

Some application language goes further and says that not only must the buyer apply for financing, he or she must also obtain a "hand-holding" letter, a document from lenders that says based on the information provided by the purchaser, he or she is qualified for a loan. The letter will then go on to say that qualification is subject to an appraisal, credit check, survey, and other standard considerations. In other words, the letter is not a loan commitment.

So why bother with a qualification letter? It provides evidence that the borrower has made a loan application and gives some sense of their ability to qualify for a loan. If a borrower cannot get a hand-holding letter from a lender, then everyone should realize the deal is unlikely to close.

Seller Take-Back. Many form agreements provide language so that a seller may take back a first or second trust. The usual content of such forms talks about rates, terms, and amounts, but sellers who use basic form language are likely to find important terms missing.

If you act as a lender then you should have available to you all the information, tools, and protections a commercial lender demands.

As a start, the loan agreement should be written in a form satisfactory to you—in other words, have your attorney pull out the right loan documents for your community and modify them as required to meet your needs.

Next, your willingness to make a loan should be conditional; that is, you must be satisfied with the borrower's credit and income. If you're not satisfied, then the deal is off.

If you're taking back a first trust, then have the buyer—at his or her expense—get a title search as well as title insurance sufficient to cover the loan amount. Have the buyer get a survey, a termite inspection—everything a commercial lender would demand.

And if it happens that the buyer is "willing" to provide loan forms, forget it. You can bet that the buyer is no dummy and the forms—no matter how formal or fancy—are filled with clauses that reduce your security.

Settlement Costs. As a seller there are certain costs you should reasonably expect to pay at closing, such as a few dollars to release a lien now on the property. But rather than go into excruciating detail about what closing costs you will or will not pay, some form agreements merely say that sellers will cover "reasonable" settlement costs.

The problem with such broad language is that the party who conducts settlement may be the buyer's lawyer and, since you are obligated to pay "reasonable fees," you may find yourself charged with many costs that the buyer might otherwise pay. The solution is to amend the agreement so that you will pay "reasonable settlement fees not to exceed $150" or whatever number seems appropriate. Speak to your attorney for specific advice.

Title. When you market real estate, you are selling a house and land, but you are selling something else as well: title that is good, merchantable, and insurable.

Good title means that the buyer will be able to finance, insure, and sell the property without difficulty. It also means that a lender will be able to do the same in the event of foreclosure.

To assure that title is good, there must be a title search. From the title search an abstract, or history, is produced, and from the abstract it is then possible to get title insurance.

Title insurance protects the buyer (and the lender) in case there are errors in the land records or if the title is clouded. For instance, if someone who owned the property 50 years ago was a habitual drunk, it's possible that he or she was not competent to sell the property to the next owner and thus the title may be clouded.

Not only does a title search cover ownership, it also looks into the matter of unpaid liens. In the usual case a home is sold free and clear of all debt, except when a loan is being assumed or the property is being bought subject to the mortgage.

Title insurance comes in two basic flavors. "Lender's" coverage protects the buyer up to the amount of loan balance, say $125,000, while "owner's" coverage protects the buyer up to the purchase price of the property—perhaps $150,000—and sometimes more. With an inflation clause, the value of owner's title insurance can rise over time if the property's value increases.

If you recently had a title search to buy or refinance, then suggest that the buyer ask about a "re-issue rate." Such a rate is sometimes available when a title search was conducted within the past five or 10 years. The re-issue rate should cut the cost of title insurance 10 to 20 percent.

Settlement. You want closing by a given date, usually 45 to 60 days after the contract is finalized.

Closing itself is nothing more than a glorified accounting of who owes what to whom. It's not a big deal and it should follow the contract provisions item for item.

Because there are contracts, there are also contractual obligations. It can happen that you have made a promise in the contract that for reasons beyond your control has not been fulfilled. For instance, you may have agreed to replace the old driveway on your Maine property with a new concrete pad, but if the contract was made in December and you have settlement in February, there's no way to thaw the earth and do a proper job in mid-winter.

The work will have to be done after closing, but how does the buyer know you will pay for the job? The buyer doesn't, and the result is that the settlement provider will set up an "escrow" account from the money coming to you at closing to assure that the work is completed by a certain date. You will receive a check for the unused balance if the job can be done without exhausting the escrow account.

Fixtures. It's usually agreed that anything attached to the house and intended to be a part of it is a "fixture," something that is to remain after a home sale. "Personalty" includes items that are in the house but are not permanently attached or intended for inclusion in the sale. The typical example is that a built-in microwave oven conveys with the property and is a fixture, while a countertop model is personalty and does not remain after the sale.

The catch to fixtures and personalty is that anything can be defined one way or the other—but only in the contract. Form agreements commonly list items expected to remain with the property, including refrigerators, wall-to-wall carpeting, shades, etc. However, if the contract says the sellers have the right to take the refrigerator with them, then the refrigerator belongs to the sellers.

The rule for fixtures is simple: if you want something to go with you after the sale and there is the remotest possibility that it could be considered a fixture, list it in the contract as an item that is not included in the transaction.

Agency. Whether a broker handles the sale or not, a standardized form will surely provide room to recognize the use of a real estate professional. The contract will identify the broker who has listed the property, and also the broker who has brought in a buyer and acted as a subagent.

If the purchaser has been represented by a buyer broker, that fact will usually be established with an addendum to the agreement. Should you see a standardized form that provides for the payment of a buyer broker without the need to attach an addendum, beware. You are probably look-ing at a pro-buyer form, a form that either should not be used or should be modified appropriately.

Also in the agency area is a very important concession by the broker.

When you hired the broker, you agreed to pay for professional services when the broker found a buyer who was "ready, able, and willing" to pay for the property. It could be argued that once a buyer has a hand-holding letter, the broker's obligations have been met and, right then and there, a commission is due.

But as a practical matter you may not have funds to pay a broker until the house goes to closing. For this reason, sales agreements typically state that as a courtesy, payment of the brokerage fee will be delayed until set-tlement.

The material on agency is also likely to contain language that greatly favors the broker in the event of certain disputes. The form might say, for example, the broker and the broker's agents will not be responsible for the condition of the property or the performance of the buyer or seller to fulfill contract terms and that the buyer cannot rely on oral statements made by the broker or the broker's agents.

Notices. Notices represent a form of contract housekeeping that can be extremely important. Suppose the agreement says the buyer must tell you within 10 calendar days if the property has received a satisfactory struc-tural inspection. How can everyone know that the message was sent and received?

The material on notices will provide a system to assure that everyone is in sync. For instance, the contract may provide that all letters sent by first-class mail will be regarded as received within three days. Or, the con-tract may say that notices must be delivered by hand or by certified mail, with a return receipt required in either case.

Adjustments. At the time you sell your home, it is entirely possible that you have prepaid local property taxes or that oil remains in the storage tank. Such matters have value and the contract will allow the settlement provider to make adjustments so that you get a credit for tax prepay-ments, oil in the tank, or whatever.

Deeds. Deeds represent evidence that you are transferring a bundle of rights to a new owner. A complex subject, deeds outline the benefits of ownership the buyer is about to receive, such matters as free and clear title, and the right to "quiet enjoyment" (a phrase that means the former owner has given up all title claims and that no one else has any title claims, either).

Deeds can also outline restrictions. For instance, an old deed may say that a bar can't be located on the premises or that commercial activity is forbidden. It may seem absurd, but bizarre deed restrictions can be enforceable, still another reason for a solid title search.

There are, however, some deed restrictions that violate public policy and are not enforceable. As examples, old deeds sometimes barred sales to blacks, Indians, and "Assyrians"—a term meant to exclude Jews.

In addition to requiring sellers to provide a deed, standardized forms also provide that buyers must record their new deed as quickly as possible. This task is done by the party handling settlement.

Insurance. Real estate contracts have one of two views when it comes to the matter of property insurance. Some forms provide that the property shall be insured by the seller until the new title is recorded. Other forms say the buyer is responsible.

If your form says that you, as a seller, are responsible for fire, theft, and liability insurance coverage until recordation, then work with your insurance agent to assure that such coverage is in force for as long as it takes to record a new title—even if you must continue the policy for a week or so after closing.

The reason you want to maintain coverage is that a deal may close on Monday but only be recorded in the public records on Friday. If the place burns down on Wednesday and you were responsible for insurance, guess who pays for all damages? The bottom line: do not cancel insurance coverage on the day of closing just to save a few premium dollars.

Possession. When a home is sold, it's expected that the seller and the seller's possessions will be gone as of closing. If the seller stays beyond closing, then a contract will typically provide that the owner is a "tenant by sufferance," meaning that he has no right to be on the property.

It sometimes happens that a seller would like to stay after settlement or a buyer would like to move in before closing. Neither event should be taken lightly. After all, what happens if the buyer moves in before closing and the loan never comes through?

Brokers and/or attorneys, as appropriate, can provide pre-settlement and post-settlement occupancy agreements, addenda that outline the conditions and obligations of early or late possession. *Do not allow your buyers to move onto the property without an appropriate agreement*, especially if you live in a community with rent control. Allow buyers, if possible, to "occupy" a property rather than "rent" it if you live in a rent-control area.

The other aspect of a possession clause is that a seller is often obligated to clean up all building violations before closing.

Condition. Probably no item stirs more passions than the usual contract clause concerning condition.

A condition clause routinely says that a seller will leave the property "free and clear of debris," "broom clean," and that all electric, heating, and air-conditioning systems will be in "working condition."

So, does this mean you have to clean out the bathtub or the oven? Is there a difference between "operating" condition and "good operating" condition?

Prior to settlement the buyer will have an opportunity for a final inspection of the property. You can imagine that at this moment a clean and attractive home will do much to raise the buyer's sense of joy. Help out and make certain the property is clean and that all debris have been hauled away.

In many areas condition clauses are taking on a new form, a detailed list signed by the seller stating that various components of the home are in working order and satisfactory condition.

Such forms are designed to reduce broker liability in case a hidden defect is found, but they raise a serious issue for sellers: are you qualified to answer questions about the condition of your own home?

For instance, do you know if the roof leaks? When was the last time you conducted a timber-by-timber inspection of the attic? Suppose an ounce of water leaks into the attic each year. Does this mean the roof leaks? Sure. Does this mean the leak is significant? That is not so certain.

As detailed condition statements become more common, sellers should protect their interests with a clause of their own, one that gives notice to buyers and declares that while you have completed the form to the best of your ability, you are not—unless otherwise stated—an architect, engineer, plumber, electrician, or carpenter and that your opinions are not a substitute for a professional structural inspection. Such a clause, as the expression goes, can't hurt and it may help considerably in the event of a dispute.

"As-Is" Sales. It is entirely appropriate to sell a home in "as-is" condition and without warranty as to its condition or workmanship. But stating that a home is being sold "as is" can mean a lower price and also make the marketing process more difficult.

If you are considering an "as-is" sale, be certain to review the matter with a broker or attorney, as appropriate, before placing your house on the market. Individual states may have specific rules relating to "as-is" sales, including what can be sold without warranty, what must be guaranteed, and also how the term "as is" must be expressed in a contract to be valid. For instance, the term "as is" may have to be capitalized or placed in quotation marks, otherwise the contract may be voidable by the purchaser.

Also, if you're selling "as is," be aware that different rules may apply to "new" and "existing" properties. It may be possible for a home with extensive improvements to be regarded as "new" in some situations, and thus subject to a somewhat different set of "as-is" requirements.

Plat. A plat is a map outlining local land holdings. In some jurisdictions there may be a requirement for the buyer to see a plat prior to closing, and a plat clause commonly says that yes, the buyer has reviewed the plat.

Termites. Despite cartoons to the contrary, termites and other wood-boring insects are not capable of destroying a home in minutes. They can damage homes over a lengthy period, however, and an infestation must be treated by the seller as a condition of settlement. The seller may also be required to repair "visible" termite damage.

Termite repairs are a tricky matter. As a seller you want to assure that your obligation to make repairs is limited to a given amount, say $500 or whatever is appropriate in your situation. If the damage exceeds your repair obligation, then the buyer should have the opportunity to back out of the deal without penalty.

The termite inspection is typically ordered and paid for by the purchaser and it is important to coordinate termite checks with lenders. Some lenders want a termite certificate delivered to them prior to closing, while others will wait. Make certain your buyer follows the lender's instructions.

Credit. When the sale is financed, somebody will want to check the buyer's credit and other financial matters. A credit clause provides full authority to obtain a credit report.

Warranties. Whether a contract form says so or not, when you sell a home you make certain promises to a buyer.

A home is, or should be, a place where people can live. So when you sell a home you make an "implied" warranty that what you are selling is properly constructed, habitable, and "reasonably fit" for use as a house.

Another form of promise is the "imposed" warranty, government rules and regulations that establish standards or requirements for certain products and services. For example, an existing home, no matter how old, may be required to have adequate fire protection, a standard that may mean all resale properties must be equipped with working smoke detectors.

A final type of warranty is the "express" warranty, a written promise generally used to limit liability. A seller, for example, might promise that the central air-conditioning system will work for at least one year after the sale. An escrow account will be established to underwrite any necessary repairs. Notice that by creating such an express warranty, the seller has not promised that the air-conditioning system will work in 18 months.

Merger. A real estate contract is an important document, yet for legal purposes it can disappear once a new deed is issued through a process called "merger." Since the contract no longer exists, its terms and promises also disappear. This may be good news for sellers, but buyers typically prefer contract language that states the contract will "survive" and not be merged into the deed.

Condos, Co-ops, and PUD. When a single-family detached home is sold, it is typically an example of "fee-simple" real estate, the highest and best form of real estate because owners have the largest possible bundle of rights. Other forms of real estate ownership, such as condos, co-ops, and private unit developments (PUDs), have fewer rights. To understand exactly what is being purchased with property that is not fee simple, buyers commonly have the right to examine ownership papers for a period of several days, during which time they may back out of a deal without penalty.

If you have something other than fee-simple property, make certain you have all required documentation in hand prior to placing your home on the market. In this way the appropriate papers will be ready for a prospective buyer.

Since the review period only begins upon receipt of the documents, it follows that sellers will want to distribute paperwork as soon as possible and that an appropriate, dated receipt should be required.

Timeshares. Timeshare units can be marketed in the same manner as one might sell real estate, but special considerations are likely to apply.

The most important timeshare issue is the matter of ownership. Some timeshare units represent a deeded real estate interest, but some time-share plans are merely "right-to-use" arrangements.

The catch to "right-to-use" arrangements is that they generally have a limited time frame, say 10 to 40 years, so that as a seller you must be certain to disclose that the "property" is not real estate in the usual sense and that only so many years of use remain before the value of what you have ends.

Also, be aware that some timeshares may not be salable, such as so-called "vacation licenses," which may give you access to a hotel or resort for a limited number of years.

Individual states have varying timeshare disclosure requirements that must be met. As with condos, co-ops, and PUDs, have all required papers in hand at the time a deal is struck, provide them to your buyer, and get a receipt because if there is a review period, it can only begin at the time all required papers are received.

Be careful when discussing tax advantages for timeshares. Simply put, there may not be any write-offs unless the property is a deeded real estate interest and the financing is secured by the property. Rather than giving tax advice, tell the buyer to check with a CPA, tax attorney, or enrolled agent for specific tax information.

Reasonable Repairs. Buried in many form agreements is a clause that states that sellers agree to make any "reasonable" repairs required by a lender. The thinking behind such language is that FHA and VA lenders may require certain repairs before financing a property. For sellers, the issue is that no one knows what is "reasonable," and therefore it may make sense to cap repair obligations, say "reasonable repairs not to exceed $1,000 in cost." If the repairs are more expensive, then the seller should have the right to back out of the deal.

Related Papers. In addition to the offer form itself, several additional forms are likely to be required, or desired.

One item is a "buyer qualification sheet," a form where the buyer describes his or her financial situation in terms of income, debts, and assets. This form basically parallels the information given to a lender, and thus allows sellers and their brokers to judge whether or not an offer is financially plausible, or to compare the financial capacity of bidders.

Basic Contract Checklist

°1) What is the price?	$_____
2) How big is the deposit?	$_____
3) Whose form is being used?	_____
4) How is the deal to be financed?	
Percent down	_____
Loan amount	$_____
Interest rate	_____
5) Maximum cash value of points from seller?	$_____
6) When must the buyer apply for a loan?	_____
7) How much cash is the buyer putting into the deal?	$_____
8) When is closing?	_____
9) Must seller make repairs?	_____
If yes, is there a limit on costs?	$_____
10) Any special fixture requirements?	_____
11) What is the real estate commission?	$_____
12) Have all required papers been delivered to the buyer?	_____
If so, do you have a receipt?	_____
13) Are there addenda?	_____
14) Are you being asked to finance all or part of the transaction?	_____
°15) Has the deal been reviewed by your attorney and/or broker, as appropriate?	_____

A smart buyer will understand that a qualification sheet is both necessary and potentially damaging. For instance, a financial information sheet that shows a buyer has a good income may cause sellers to bargain for more money or better terms because they know the buyer can pay a higher price.

To limit damage, a savvy buyer will complete the sheet in a way that is both literally correct and yet not too revealing. For example, if a buyer needs an annual income of $50,000 to qualify for a loan but actually makes $75,000 a year, the qualification sheet may show the purchaser's income as being "$50,000 plus."

ADDENDA

Having gone through a list of the items that one might expect to encounter in a standardized form agreement, and recognizing that if certain items are missing sellers should be concerned, we now turn to an even wider universe of issues: the subjects that can be added to a form agreement.

If someone hands you a form, it is possible to change the wording and meaning by adding language or crossing out offensive wording. It is also possible to simply add a page or two of nicely typed language that accomplishes whatever needs to be done.

To have a successful addendum, or rider, it is necessary to consider six important issues.

1) Does the main contract say that one or more addenda are attached? If not, it should.

2) The addenda should be numbered to show how many pages have been added to the agreement. For example, page 1 would be marked as "Page 1 of 3 Pages."

3) The property should be identified on each addendum page.

4) There should be a clear statement explaining the role of the addendum, a sentence or paragraph making it clear that the language in the addendum is to take precedence over any conflicting or contrary language found in the main body of the contract, or any previous riders.

5) There must be the addendum itself, the special language you want as part of the contract.

6) There must be a signature block so that *each* addendum is signed and dated by each party to the agreement.

Addenda are enormously important because they can clarify certain negotiating issues with a precision and slant not found in form agreements.

Perhaps the most common rider is a structural inspection clause. You're selling a home and the buyer wants to make certain that the home is in good physical condition. As a seller you *want* the buyer to have an inspection because it will then become tremendously difficult for the buyer to later claim that you hid damage or a dangerous condition.

So the buyer says, "I want a structural inspection." You say fine, *provided the buyer gives you a copy of the structural inspection and any related documents.*

A basic inspection clause will say, yes, "Buyer Jones shall have the right to a structural inspection by the inspector of his choice and at his cost." The clause does not commit you to make repairs if damage is found, and it does not say the buyer can get out of the deal if repairs are needed. In effect, the clause offers information to the buyer rather than protection.

Less attractive—at least from the seller's perspective—is language that says you will repair such damage as may be found. The problem here is that there is no cap on costs and no limit on your obligation to perfect the property. Potentially you could be forced to fix a scratch or replace the entire roof. Inspection clauses that create unlimited seller liability are clearly unacceptable.

A better choice is to have repair caps. For instance, you should not be required to make repairs with an individual cost of less than $100 or more than $500, or whatever numbers are appropriate. With caps, small items can be ignored and if the dollar amount of repair costs exceeds the cap, then you can pay the extra expense or the buyer can quit the deal without penalty.

And so it goes, back and forth, until acceptable language is developed.

In the process of creating an addendum it is likely that a smart buyer will insist that the inspection must be "satisfactory" to him or her, that the inspector is selected by the purchaser, and that a reasonable period is allowed in which to conduct the inspection, say seven calendar days after the contract is accepted. If the review is not satisfactory, then the deal is finished and the buyer's deposit must be returned.

The term "satisfactory" is a loaded expression because your view of satisfactory and the buyer's may differ. Satisfaction, for example, can be any reasonable standard set by a buyer, no matter how unreasonable the standard may seem to you.

Whether the rider is for a structural inspection, legal review, termite inspection, or whatever, *when a deal is dependent on a buyer's "satisfaction," an option has been created*. The property may be satisfactory or unsatisfactory, but you cannot sell the property to anyone else because the purchaser is first in line to buy—or not buy—your house. If the buyer views the property as "unsatisfactory," then a properly written contingency will allow him or her to back out of the deal without penalty.

What can you do to limit a "satisfaction" option? If the option is within reason, say a few days to inspect a property or have an attorney review the papers, accept it as part of the bargaining process. If the review period is overly long, then argue for a shorter option time, or do not agree to the deal.

If a buyer comes back with additional legal language or changes in the contract form, check the wording with caution and review the matter with your lawyer.

You must be careful because language that looks dull and harmless may well have a specific legal meaning that greatly damages your position. You don't have to accept new language or conditions, but if you do, be certain you understand what is being said and presume that any new wording is there to benefit the buyer.

Structural inspections, legal reviews, and similar provisions should be seen as clauses that effectively create an option on your property at little cost or discomfort to the buyer. There is nothing inherently wrong with allowing a short-term option, especially when sales are slow.

But in a hot seller's market with a line of buyers outside the door, you may be able to demand a shorter option term (say five days rather than 10) and language more suited to your bargaining position. Or, as sellers sometimes do when they have the upper hand, simply reject any deal with a contingency.

14
Judging Offers

The moment will come, as it does three to four million times a year, when someone will say, "That's the house for me" and hand you or your broker a written offer.

Is it the right offer? Dare you change its terms?

Before looking at the fine print, consider these important points.

- An offer can be withdrawn any time prior to acceptance. You must respond quickly if your intent is to accept.
- If you modify any number, word, or phrase, the offer is dead and you have made a counter-offer. This is good news if the buyer accepts your response, but the buyer is neither compelled to accept your response nor to continue with the original offer. Thus modifying offers is not a casual event.
- If an offer is rejected there is no way to tell when another offer will be made, if ever. There are cases where owners have turned down an offer because it was marginally low and then watched as their homes sat on the market for months and years.
- Once a written contract has been accepted by buyers and sellers, it can only be modified with the agreement of all parties. In effect, a deal is a deal in real estate, so everyone benefits by getting it right the first time.

In evaluating offers one must start from the position that the probability of getting everything you want is unlikely. To score perfectly you need a hot market, a great house, an unbeatable location, terrific financing, and a breathless buyer. It can happen, but odds are that it won't.

If you haven't been able to pocket that perfect offer, then an offer must be analyzed in terms of its "musts," "shoulds," and "extras."

"Musts" are things you absolutely have to have. If a price below $285,000 means you can't buy the next home, then no matter how wonderful $275,000 may appear, it won't work.

"Shoulds" are things you would like to have, but life will go on without them. Yes, it would be great to have the buyer pay all points, but paying one point may not be so terrible in the context of a given sale.

"Extras" are the things that come with a deal that you did not expect but are delighted to have. You mean the buyer will take the place without forcing you to replace the old roof? Great. Don't argue.

Once you get past the musts, shoulds, and extras it's time to look at the details.

- What's your net benefit?

This is a critical question that can be used to quickly analyze the finances of the entire deal.

For instance, Tessler is selling his home for $385,000. Newmont offers $360,000, but the deal is structured so that Tessler will not walk away from closing with $360,000. The offer says Tessler must pay one point, $3,000 in this case because Newmont wants a $300,000 loan. Tessler is supposed to fix the roof ($8,000), repair the pool ($2,000), pay 50 percent of all transfer taxes ($2,500 in the jurisdiction where the property is located), and pay the first $3,000 of Newmont's closing expenses.

Running the numbers, the deal requires Tessler to pay $18,500 in expenses plus a 6 percent real estate commission ($21,600), or a total of $40,100. Net benefit: $319,900.

It may be that $319,900 is acceptable to Tessler. The important point is that within the deal is a variety of costs and expenses that make the proposed pact worth substantially less than $360,000—and a lot less than $385,000.

- Are there gotcha clauses?

A real estate sale is a complex transaction and an offer today is likely to contain a variety of contingencies.

A typical, and acceptable, contingency concerns financing. A form agreement will commonly say that if the buyer cannot get the financing outlined in the offer, then the deal is off and the buyer's deposit is to be returned.

Such clauses make sense for everyone. As a seller, you don't want the house tied up and unsalable for months while an unqualified buyer runs around to 700 loan offices.

There may also be "gotcha" clauses (as in: we got you) that should trigger great curiosity. No-money-down deals need to be examined carefully to see what risk, if any, is on the shoulders of the buyer. Offers that demand seller financing with substitution or subordination clauses should be rejected out of hand. Deals completed on forms conveniently supplied by the purchaser, or by a buyer broker, must be examined word for word.

• Is the buyer capable?

The best offer in the world is worthless if the buyer cannot follow through. As an example, if Lexington wants to buy a home and is heir to a $5-million trust fund, that's great—as long as the money is available. If the trustee has other plans for the money and cannot be compelled to release the funds, then Lexington's offer is worthless.

All offers should require buyers to apply for financing within seven to 10 calendar days, and present evidence (a hand-holding letter) within that time frame showing they are generally qualified to finance the deal.

Habitual drunks, drug users, lunatics, bigamists, and those who are senile may not have the legal capacity to enter into contracts. Minors may enter into contracts to which they are not bound—but you are.

• Is the deal plausible?

It sometimes happens that a buyer wants a property but must first eliminate one or more barriers before a deal can be completed.

A common example is the case of house number 1. In this situation, Fawcett wants your home but to raise the down payment and qualify for a loan must first sell the property he has, a home that happens to be in a community left behind by industry and business. Fawcett may be the nicest fellow in the world, but his offer is only possible if he sells *and* settles house number 1—a great improbability.

The Fawcetts of the world can be dealt with through adroit contracting. You might say, for example, that Fawcett has a deal, but if you receive another offer Fawcett has 24 hours to rid his offer of all contingencies and close the deal or else his offer is null and void, his deposit will be returned in full, and you can sell the property to the new buyers who hold a backup agreement. Fawcett is likely to accept such an arrangement because it means he cannot be caught with two houses—and two mortgages.

• Should you tinker?

An offer is an offer until you change it. Then it becomes a counter-offer.

In weighing offers you must consider what is important, and what

Finding Mr. Tessler's Net Benefit	
Sale Price	$360,000
Less One Point	3,000
Roof	8,000
Pool	2,000
Transfer Taxes	2,500
Newmont's Closing Costs	3,000
Real Estate Commission	21,600
Total Costs	40,100
Net Benefit	$319,900

isn't. An offer, for example, may require you to replace the kitchen disposal, an item that might cost $200. While the idea of spending several hundred dollars may not be too exciting, such a cost must be viewed within the context of the overall deal. If the house is selling for $200,000 and the buyers want a $200 concession, make it. Remember that if you refuse a $200 repair you are asking that the buyers modify their offer, which means it's dead and you may never get another one. For $200 it just isn't worth the risk.

Other items may not be so understandable. If the property is selling for $200,000 and the buyers want you to spend $5,000 to fix the roof, there is a significant expense on the table. Do you take the offer or not? One step, certainly, is to contact several roofers to see if the job can be done more cheaply.

• Have you set aside concessions?

Everyone likes to feel good in the bargaining process and for this reason it's often important to have a few "gimmes" to throw into a deal.

You might list your home for sale with the stipulation that the washer and dryer will not convey, even though you don't want them because your new home comes equipped with such appliances. If Wilson comes along and offers $135,000 but you want $137,000, you might then say to Wilson, "Look, raise your price to $137,000 and you can have the washer and dryer. You know, I wanted to take them with me but if it will make the deal better for you, I'll go along with it." Wilson need not know that you didn't want the washer and dryer.

• What are your alternatives?

Whatever offer you receive must be judged on the basis of such options as may be available.

It is entirely possible that no alternative is available, that the offer in hand—no matter how bleak—is the best choice. That can be an unfortunate reality in areas where homes aren't selling but owners must move.

Another choice is that a given offer is so bad that you would be better off keeping your home and either using it as a residence or as a rental property. This, too, may not be a happy circumstance, but it may be the best option.

If you elect to rent a personal residence, be certain to first speak with a tax professional because valuable advantages may be lost by renting.

The best possible situation is to have an alternative, to have two offers on the table. This can be a delightful experience, assuming both are attractive.

The probability that two offers will be exactly alike in every detail is remote, so there is rarely a situation where one can only decide by tossing a coin. But if it happens that the two offers are very close, and if they are also attractive, which do you choose?

Suppose you're asking $285,000 and two offers come in at $279,950 with 20 percent down and no points for you to pay.

One test is surely the ability of each prospective buyer to complete the deal. The buyer with the larger income and better credit should get the nod, because the odds are that they will have an easier time obtaining financing.

If the deals are *similar* and the qualifications of the buyers are relatively equal, then the next step is to consider the source of each offer. If one was brought in by your listing broker, and you like your listing broker, and the other was brought in by a broker you don't know, then you can choose the offer that came through the lister.

The situation is different if the property is priced at $285,000 and two offers for that amount come in. Assuming that both offers precisely meet the listing agreement, the first one wins.

• What is the cost of saying no?

If we accept a given offer, we know what we will receive. But is there a cost if we say no?

Economists say that every decision, whether yes or no, embodies certain "opportunity costs." If we say no to an offer from Mr. Hyde, our property will remain unsold. We will have to make additional mortgage and tax payments. We will not have the equity in the property that can only be released through a sale. We will not be able to move as quickly as we want, and while we wait interest rates may rise—a factor that will make our place harder to sell and our next home more expensive.

Moreover, if we say no to Mr. Hyde's first offer there may not be a second one. It's also possible that no one else will make an offer.

Nothing is without risk or cost, something to consider when evaluating an offer.

- Should you shop an offer?

In this situation you're selling the home for $108,000, you have an offer for $103,000, and there is a second potential buyer looking at the property. You would like to have a second offer, just to see if it is more attractive than the first. Can you tell the second set of buyers about the first offer?

You certainly can say that you've received a written offer that is now being considered, but you can't show anyone the offer because it would violate the buyer's privacy. Because the second purchasers can't see the offer, they may not believe it exists.

Also, the second set of buyers may be cowed by the thought that they do not want to get into a bidding war, especially when they don't know what the other side is bidding or if another side exists.

Will the second set of buyers believe you or your broker? If everyone has been treated fairly in the marketing and bargaining process, the answer is likely to be yes. But if there has been the slightest inappropriate remark, the most minor evasion, then the second set of buyers is likely to be quizzical at best, unbelieving at worst.

- What about the "maybe" buyer?

In no case is it ethical or appropriate to state that an offer has been received when that is not the case. But a less certain matter concerns the "maybe" buyer.

A maybe buyer is someone who might be interested in the property, and thus a possible bidder. For example, if the Raleighs are interested in your property and the Twillmans are going to see it this evening, then it's fair and appropriate to mention to the Twillmans that "we do have other buyers interested in the house and you should know that they may make an offer."

The statement above is literally true. There are other buyers (the Raleighs) who will be looking at the property and it is correct to say that they *may* make an offer. The existence of other buyers may well cause the Twillmans to act a little faster or bid a little higher.

Of course, it's equally true that the Raleighs may not make an offer, but as a negotiator it's not your job to point this out.

• What do your professionals say?

The idea is not that the opinions of professionals are without bias or self-interest, but rather that such views do not have the same psychological entanglements owners are likely to possess. This different perspective can help you sort through the values an offer may contain. Or lack.

• Are you pleased?

It sometimes happens that we don't get all we want, but life goes on.

You can't lose what you never had, a point to consider when evaluating real estate offers. Sure, we asked $195,000 for the property, and yes, the offer for $189,000 is less, but did we lose $6,000? Nobody wanted to pay $195,000 for our place, so it was never worth that much. We didn't lose $6,000. We never had it.

Sometimes there is a wondrous peace in accepting a *good* deal—certainly more peace then holding out for a *great* deal that may never come.

15
Almost Done

Once a contract has been signed, there is a both a sense of triumph and a strong urge to celebrate. But before the festivities begin, there is the grim reality that a contract is unlikely to be the end of the selling process, merely a marker along the way.

While a contract certainly represents a deal, most deals these days are conditional. Contracts say the house is sold—but only after certain hurdles have been cleared.

HURDLE 1: FINANCING

Loans, in most cases, are likely to be a priority item. While a growing number of buyers pre-qualify for financing before they start the house-hunting process, many do not.

Real estate loans are available from numerous sources, including banks, savings and loan associations, mortgage bankers, and mortgage brokers. As a seller it's not your business *where* the buyer gets a loan, only that a good-faith effort is made to obtain financing.

If your agreement requires the buyer to apply for financing within a reasonable time, say seven to ten days, then—naturally—the buyer should promptly apply for a loan and obtain a hand-holding letter. Should it happen that the buyer meets with lenders and is turned down, then the deposit should be returned and the deal ended.

If you're taking back financing, make certain you receive all required papers and information.

Deposits are a major financial issue. If you're a self-seller and the buyer needs a loan, you are certainly welcome to recommend lenders or to suggest a quick review of the phone book. What you cannot do is require a buyer to use one loan source or another, and under no condition can you receive cash or "a thing of value" for steering a buyer to a particular lender.

If you have a broker, that individual will undoubtedly know a number of loan sources, including several he or she has used in the past. The broker may prefer one lender over another, but again the buyer cannot be compelled to use a particular lender.

Real estate brokers now offer mortgage loan services and it may be very much in your broker's interest to finance the deal. If a broker can offer the best rates and terms, or rates and terms that match the best available loan from another source, that's fine. But even if your real estate broker has the most wonderful mortgages known to mankind, under no condition can the buyer be compelled to obtain financing from your broker.

There is a potential problem with brokers who provide real estate financing, a problem that should be understood.

Let's say Maynard wants to buy your home. He's a fine fellow and has scraped together every dime and nickel in his possession to win the title of "homeowner." With a loan at 8 percent from your real estate broker, Maynard can afford up to $100,000 in financing.

But your house could be worth more if Maynard went mortgage shopping elsewhere. Maybe a lender down the street from your broker has loans at 7.75 percent, an interest rate that would allow Maynard to finance $102,275 for your home.

It thus becomes very important to understand that real estate brokers who offer mortgage financing are obligated, as your agent, to place your interests first. In my view, that means brokers must make certain that a buyer consults with many loan sources before deciding to use one lender or another. If, after calling a variety of lenders, the buyer elects to finance through your broker, that's okay.

In addition, if several offers are on the table, preference should not be given to buyers who have said that if the deal goes through, they will use your real estate broker to obtain financing. Such a situation ("I'll recommend your offer only if you get a loan through me") can be construed as a "tying" arrangement and thus a big problem for a broker and potentially the party who hired the broker—you.

The bottom line: you and your broker are welcome to provide information about financing alternatives and to wish the buyer good luck. Any effort to direct a buyer to one loan source or another in exchange for compensation or remuneration should be seen for what it is: potentially illegal steering or tying that may result in substantial costs and consequences.

If a broker provides real estate financing services, it is recommended as a condition of the sale that the buyer sign a statement confirming that he or she understands and has been told that:

- The use of a particular lender is not required as a condition of the sale.
- The buyer has been advised to consult with as many loan sources as possible, including—but not limited to—savings and loan associations, commercial banks, insurance companies, credit unions, mortgage brokers, and mortgage bankers.
- If the real estate broker representing the seller, or a subagent representing the seller, offers mortgage services, the buyer's decision to use or not use such financing services shall not be a factor when judging a purchase offer.

HURDLE 2: UNFINISHED BUSINESS

A large and growing number of sales now require home inspections, and a typical contract form will give the buyer seven to 10 days to have an inspector go through the house.

You should expect that the home inspector will find a variety of small problems with your house. This is normal, reasonable, and not an issue. If larger problems are found, then you must look to the contract language to determine your obligations.

But what if the sales agreement says you will make repairs before closing and such repairs cannot be made? For instance, suppose the property is in Wisconsin, the sale is in January, and you have an air-conditioning system? There is no practical way to test the air-conditioning system and yet the buyer wants to know—without question—that the air-conditioning system works. How can you create such assurance without a test?

The answer is to create an "escrow" account (a trust account) with the settlement provider. Suppose that the largest conceivable repair for the air conditioner costs $1,000. In this case you might place $1,000 in the escrow account with the understanding that the buyer is responsible for ordering all repairs, that payments will only be made from the escrow account on the basis of written receipts, and that all money not spent by June 1 will be returned to you.

As a seller, you should view escrow accounts as a better choice than a settlement delay. But an even better solution is to take whatever steps are necessary to assure that an escrow account is not required. After all, while you may think a given repair is simple and cheap, the buyer may want to include gold-plated nuts and bolts, especially if the bill is being underwritten by money in an escrow account—money that is potentially yours.

. HURDLE 3: RENEGOTIATION

An increasingly frequent part of the negotiation process is the use of satisfaction clauses for structural inspections, legal reviews, and other matters.

To the extent that buyers want additional assurances before completing a deal, satisfaction clauses are necessary. And from a seller's viewpoint, if a buyer decides for some reason—no matter how strange or absurd—that he or she is not satisfied, it's usually better to end a deal early than to have it drag on for months and not have a sale.

For some buyers, however, a satisfaction clause often has a different purpose: it's seen as a device to renegotiate a deal.

With a pro-buyer satisfaction clause, a purchaser can come back and say, "Gee, I like your place but I cannot regard the inspection as satisfactory unless the following repairs are made." *In effect, some buyers— whether purposely or not—use option clauses to re-open negotiations.*

Do you make the repairs? In a buyer's market, probably yes because you want to close the deal. In a seller's market, maybe no because buyers abound.

The problem with renegotiation is that it is usually a selective process. The buyer wants more goodies or a lower price, but is shocked by the thought that with a different package you might want more money or better terms.

Do you renegotiate? The answer is an individual decision that depends on the market and the value of the buyer's offer. But at least be prepared for a renegotiation effort, and have a series of backup positions available if needed.

HURDLE 4: PAPERS

If you are selling a condo, co-op, or private unit development (PUD) then you are marketing a property with less than a full bundle of rights. How much less will depend on the type of property you have and the precise arrangements that govern its use, ownership, and sale.

With a condo, for example, buyers will want to see the declaration, bylaws, rules, regulations, current budget, past budget, projected budget, and perhaps the original public offering statement as well. Individual states will require you to provide selected documents and to allow the buyer adequate time to review all materials, perhaps three days from the moment of receipt. If the buyer is not happy with the papers, then he or she can generally withdraw from the deal without penalty.

As a seller you want all papers available at the time an offer is made. Upon acceptance, you or your broker should provide needed papers and you should also get a signed, dated receipt from the buyer showing that all documents have been received.

To determine your paperwork requirements, consult with a knowledgeable broker or real estate attorney.

Co-ops present a somewhat different set of post-contract hurdles.

Ownership in a co-op is represented by stock as well as by the exclusive right to use a portion of the property. The catch to co-op sales is that such deals commonly require approval of the co-op board before a sale can be finalized. Either you or your broker should introduce the buyer to other co-op owners and arrange for such board approval as may be required.

HURDLE 5: BUGS

If your deal involves financing, then the lender will require a careful examination of the property to determine if there are any active infestations of termites or other wood-boring insects, and to see if there is any damage.

It is your job, or the broker's, to make sure that the property is open and accessible to the inspector at a mutually convenient time. The inspector, in the wording of many contract forms, is required to check "accessible" areas of the home and look for "visible" damage, language that is something less than specific.

If you have an active infestation, lenders will require treatment prior to closing. If there is damage, you may or may not have to make repairs, depending on the wording in your sales agreement. If repair work is necessary it must be done prior to settlement or an escrow account will be required.

HURDLE 6: THE APPRAISAL

A crucial player in the post-contract period is the appraiser, an individual paid by the purchaser but selected by the lender to evaluate the market value of the house.

In most situations if a property is fairly typical and the price is within the range of reason, the appraiser will value the property at the price accepted by both the buyer and seller.

However, there are situations where the appraiser will not agree with the sales price. If the appraisal is higher than the sale price, then you as a seller may have a tinge of remorse but the deal will go through.

If the appraised value is below the sale price, then there are problems.

If the contract says the house is worth $245,000 and the borrower wants 90 percent financing, that means a $220,500 loan is required to make the deal work. But if the property is appraised at $235,000, then the maximum mortgage a lender will provide with 90 percent financing is $211,500. If the property is to be sold at $245,000, the buyer will need a down payment of $33,500 rather than $24,500.

What to do? Sellers need to think through low appraisals with great care.

One choice is to speak with the appraiser and discuss the valuation. Are there important items that have been left out or undervalued? Remember that the appraiser is the professional, so ask nicely.

An alternative option is to seek a field review in the case of an FHA loan, or to have the loan underwriter visit the property.

A last choice is to get a second appraiser through the lender and see if better numbers show up.

If the low appraisal stands, then sellers must make a decision. One option is to say the price is firm, in which case the buyer can probably opt out of the deal without penalty because needed financing is not available.

A compromise, if possible, might work like this: you'll lower the price somewhat if the buyer will raise the down payment.

The last alternative is to lower the selling price to the appraised value. This is hardly the world's best choice, but consider that without the current buyer you'll need a replacement, a commodity that may be in limited supply. And even if you get another buyer, perhaps the same problem will arise.

Three hints:

1) Make the home available when the appraiser wants to see it.

2) Have the place in show condition to get a top valuation.

3) If you don't like the appraisal, have the buyer (who paid for it) supply a copy of the report for your review. Under Section 701(e) of the Equal Credit Opportunity Act of 1991, if requested by a mortgage loan applicant, a lender must furnish a copy of the appraisal report used to value residential real estate.

HURDLE 7: PROPERTY INSURANCE

The property must always be insured, and as a seller it is advisable for you to maintain insurance through closing and until the title transfer is actually recorded in local land records.

Some contract forms say the buyer is responsible for insurance at closing. But what if the place burns down and the buyer's insurance is inadequate or magically not in force? For the few dollars involved, it pays to maintain insurance until recordation and legal title is held by the purchaser.

A related matter concerns lender insurance requirements. Some lenders want insurance policies from buyers before closing, while others want a policy at closing. Avoid surprises and advise the buyer to ask about the lender's requirements when applying for a loan.

HURDLE 8: THE WALK-THROUGH

Prior to closing, the buyer has a final opportunity to walk through the property, an inspection that is often misunderstood.

When the contract was signed, the property was sold subject to various contingencies—financing, inspections, whatever. Within the deal was an understanding that the property was sold in the condition it was in at the time the contract was signed. But you are likely to occupy the property for a month or two after the contract is created and it follows that during this period nothing should be done to damage the house.

The walk-through is intended to assure that the home is in substantially the same condition at closing as it was when the contract was signed. If there was a broken piece of glass at the time the contract was signed, then unless there was an agreement to the contrary, that is how the house was sold.

But just before closing the home no longer has furnishings, pictures, or rugs. Every flaw in the house is magnified and the buyers, already nervous, may well complain about a series of minor matters.

Protect yourself. Immediately after the contract is signed, get a camera and photograph every room and the outside of the property. In particular, photograph mars, cracks, carpet stains, holes in the walls, and every other minor dent and bulge that could become a closing issue. Have the photos developed by a lab that places a date stamp on the back, if possible.

Bring your photos to closing, but do not show them to anyone unless a walk-through problem emerges.

Alternatively, if the piano movers scrape the wall the day you moved out, tell the buyers. In most cases they intend to repaint anyway and will dismiss the matter as inconsequential—but only if you bring it up first.

16
Closing

If there is a pot of gold at the end of the marketing process, closing is where you'll find it.

Real estate settlements are regarded as mystic rites by many, an unfathomable array of activities and documents held together with hidden codes and secret understandings.

Settlement is complex for the simple reason that it's not a daily event for most people. Money, contracts, deeds, title, and large mounds of paperwork are tangled together because many interests and issues are being resolved simultaneously.

Closing can also be an adversarial event where otherwise civil buyers and sellers lunge at one another in an effort to mangle important body parts held dear by the opposition. Yelling, crying, debate, fights, and armed duels are not unknown, but the good news is that you are unlikely to witness such conflict.

Why?

My usual explanation works this way: a real estate contract is like the script for a play, the buyers and sellers are actors, and closing is nothing more than the play itself. If a script is properly written, the play will go off without trouble and the same concept applies to a real estate deal. If you've followed the advice given earlier in this guide, worked carefully with local professionals, and anticipated problems, then a solid contract should make closing a relaxed event lasting anywhere from 30 minutes to an hour.

Closing practices vary around the country, but one point is constant: many people are interested in the process. Brokers want to be paid, governments want their taxes, lawyers want their fees, buyers want their property, and sellers want a check. In effect, closing is the place to sort out claims, make payments, and finish the deal.

REPRESENTATION

Part of the mystery that surrounds closing involves the very special issue of representation.

If you have had a broker or attorney in the selling process, they have worked for you, but with closing the relationship between you and your professionals may not be so clear or certain.

Those who handle settlements commonly regard themselves as "agents" of the settlement process, neutral beings who are there merely to apportion money and favors as directed by the sales contract. If there is a dispute, it's up to the parties to resolve the matter, not the impartial settlement provider. If you need advice, well, neutral parties cannot favor one side or the other, can they?

If, as a seller, you have been working with a broker or attorney, ask your professionals two questions: do you conduct closings? If you conduct closings will you be my representative or will you be a non-partisan agent of the settlement process?

Depending on the answers, here are your choices.

1) You get to choose the settlement agent and have your broker or lawyer handle the closing, but with the understanding that they regard themselves as neutral parties in the settlement process. In this situation you must choose another attorney to act as your representative and review all paperwork prior to closing.

2) You get to choose the closing agent and your broker or lawyer will both handle closing and represent your interests. Fine.

3) Neither your broker nor your lawyer handle closings or the buyer gets to select the settlement provider. Insist that your attorney review all paperwork prior to closing.

Because settlement providers make mistakes, and because important interests are at risk, it is always to your advantage to have a knowledgeable representative go through the paperwork before closing, or to actually attend settlement. If it seems like overkill in some cases to have a settlement provider, seller's attorney, and buyer's lawyer at the closing table, just consider what it might cost if you are not represented.

FORM EVENTS

The best way to figure out who owes what to whom is to work from the standardized government form used universally by settlement providers, the so-called HUD-1. And—since it's a government form—it makes sense to start from the back.

The HUD-1 groups issues by subject matter and each general area has a few lines on the form. Going from top to bottom, here are the transaction costs that will be found on the back of the form. For example, here's what might happen if the Muldoon house is sold for $230,000 to the Leonards.

Brokers (700 Lines). Starting from the top, the "700" items concern commissions and fees paid to real estate brokers. Line 700 shows the sale price and the percentage represented by the brokerage commission, say $230,000 and a 6 percent commission in this example.

Line 701 says the seller's broker received $6,900 and line 702 shows the cooperating broker received another $6,900. Line 703 shows the total commission, $13,800 in this example.

Loan Fees (800 Lines). The 800 items record loan costs. The loan origination fee, if any, is shown on line 801. Line 802 refers to the "loan discount," which, in English, means points. If the loan amount is $172,500, and there is one point, then each point is valued at $1,725. If the Muldoons and the Leonards agreed in their sales contract to split one point, then each will pay $862.50.

Line 803 provides for payment to the appraiser. This cost can be paid at settlement, or it may be marked "POC," an expression that means "paid out of closing."

Line 804 records payment for a credit report. As this is typically paid through the lender, the amount is usually recorded with the notation "POC."

The 800 area also includes lines for:

- The lender's inspection fee (line 805) if it was necessary to physically examine the property.
- A mortgage insurance application fee (line 806) for those who put down less than 20 percent and require mortgage insurance.
- An assumption fee (line 807) if the deal involves an assumption. Blank lines in this area can be used to record such items as a processing fee, tax service fee (so that certain information is reported to the IRS), document preparation by the settlement provider, and a flood certification (showing whether or not the property is subject to flooding).
- A processing fee for the lender to review the loan papers (line 808).

Prepaid Costs (900 Lines). You may hear about deals with small down payments except for "prepaid items," and here they are.

Line 901 concerns short-term interest on the buyer's loan. Suppose closing is on the 10th, but loan payments start on the first day of the next month. There is a 20-day period before the first true loan payment when the money is outstanding and the lender wants daily interest, an amount reflected on line 901.

Lenders require borrowers to prepay mortgage insurance (line 902) and hazard insurance (line 903) premiums to assure such policies are in effect as of closing.

Reserves (1000 Lines). Loan agreements routinely provide for lenders to make direct payments for such items as property taxes and hazard insurance. To ensure that such money is available, lenders take two steps. First, they collect one-twelfth of such costs each month and, second, they collect money up front to create a reserve account in case a payment is missed. The 1000 lines show how much reserve money is collected at closing for each item.

Title Charges (1100 Lines). When you sell a home, you are not just selling a residence. You are selling legal title and the world needs to be certain that you actually own the property and have the right to sell it. So someone goes down to the courthouse and searches the ownership history as far back as possible. A condensed version of this history, a so-called "abstract," is then created, and from the abstract it is possible to issue title insurance.

Title insurance protects against errors in the public record, information that has not been recorded, and blunders in the abstract and examination process. Lenders will require so-called "lender's" coverage to protect the property up to the value of the outstanding loan amount. In addition, buyers may wish to purchase "owner's" coverage, title insurance that gives protection up to the purchase price of the property and sometimes more if an inflation clause is included in the policy.

Buried in the title-insurance premium is often a commission to the party conducting settlement. How much of a commission? One survey showed that commissions amounted to 32 to 72 percent of the premium amount. How much is paid out in claims? Eight to twelve cents on the dollar, according to one report.

It's title-insurance premiums that explain why some lawyers and title

What's a RESPA?

Virtually all closings in the United States are governed by the Real Estate Settlement and Procedures Act of 1974 as amended, a law now universally known as "RESPA."

RESPA is important to sellers because it contains a variety of requirements that must be met to have a proper closing.

All closings must use the uniform settlement sheet developed by the Department of Housing and Urban Development (HUD). This means closing costs and fees are broken up in a standardized manner, so they are possibly more understandable than might otherwise be the case.

Buyers and sellers can require settlement providers to supply final closing figures "during the business day immediately preceding the day of settlement." In English, you—or your broker or attorney—can review the numbers before closing to check for errors and omissions.

Under RESPA, kickbacks and unearned fees are illegal. "Naked" referrals are banned, deals where Smith gives your name to Jones, Jones originates your mortgage, and then pays a fee or "thing of value" to Smith.

For buyers, RESPA requires lenders to provide a good-faith estimate of closing costs within three days of placing a loan application. "Good faith" does not mean absolutely accurate, but it does mean a solid, reasonable ballpark estimate. Lenders must also provide borrowers with a guide from HUD explaining the settlement process.

companies conduct closing for $199 or whatever figure is currently hot. The big money is not in the closing fee, it's hidden in the title-insurance premium.

Some state bar associations feel that attorneys should not receive title-insurance commissions because no selling is involved (where else can the buyer get title coverage?) and few, if any, legal skills are needed to fill in the blanks on title-insurance forms. Other bar associations feel that collecting title-insurance premiums is acceptable.

Sorting through title-insurance matters raises four important issues.

1) Lenders require title insurance, so buyers must have it.

2) A settlement provider who sells title insurance cannot provide advice without actual or potential bias. Title coverage varies and buyers should have an independent information source, one reason buyers should have a lawyer at closing.

3) If a home has been bought or refinanced within the past five to ten years, it may be possible to get a "re-issue" rate and save 10 to 20 per-

cent. It's something you can suggest to buyers, if you like them.

4) There is a serious need to review the entire title-insurance industry, and to see if it is effectively regulated, fairly priced, and even necessary. In this review process it is worth mentioning that title insurance is not sold in Iowa and yet, somehow, mortgages are made.

Is title insurance an issue for sellers? Not directly. But if you're selling a house today the probability is that you will be buying tomorrow, which means you should know how the title-insurance system works.

Line 1107 is reserved for attorney fees, meaning the attorney who conducts closing. This fee should include the cost of such services as title insurance document preparation and a title examination.

Taxes (1200 Lines). Some of the largest expenses associated with closing can be found in this area. State and local governments have discovered that real estate sales are an ideal revenue source because various fees and charges don't have the look, feel, or political impact of income taxes or sales taxes. The result is that transfer fees have been steadily rising even as politicians remind voters of their efforts to hold down pesky income taxes.

Tax figures should be checked with care and settlement providers should be asked if any reductions or exemptions are available for the purchase of residential property or for buyers above a certain age.

Miscellaneous (1300 Lines). This is where you can find charges for surveys and termite inspections. It is also where a new and growing expense can be found, the cost of overnight and express delivery services. Delivery services should be reviewed with care to ensure that you are not paying more than actual costs.

Total Settlement Charges (Line 1400). Add up everything on the page and the individual totals for buyers and sellers will appear on line 1400.

For sellers, the back of a HUD-1 is likely to be fairly blank. The largest likely expenses will be for brokerage services, if any, followed by a charge for points. A few miscellaneous bills for preparing a deed release and messenger fees are likely to round out most seller expenses.

Line 1400 lets you see how all the people who did not buy and did not sell—the brokers, lawyers, lenders, and all the rest—benefited from your deal.

FRONT OF THE FORM

Having gone through the back of the form, it's now possible to get to more interesting numbers, those found on the front of the HUD-1.

The front of the form is organized into a side for the buyer and a side for the seller. At the top is general information showing who conducted closing, the names of buyers, sellers, and lenders, and the file number, loan number, and mortgage insurance case number. These numbers can be extremely important if there is a need to review the transaction in the future, say in the event of a tax audit, insurance claim, or estate matter.

Be certain to place closing papers in a safe place and do not throw them out. Ever.

Buyer's Summary and Adjustments (100 Lines). Here you will find the sale price (line 101) as well as transaction costs from line 1400 on the back of the form.

Also in this area are adjustments. For example, you may have prepaid local taxes. At closing you will then receive a credit for prepaid taxes, an amount added to the borrower's closing costs.

Adjustments can involve any home-related item you have prepaid, including taxes, assessments, and condo fees. Adjustments can also be made for noncash items. For instance, if you have an oil furnace, you also have an oil tank. Whatever remains in the tank can be an adjustable item. Line 120, a heart-stopper for buyers at many closings, provides the total cost of the deal before credits.

Buyer Credits and Adjustments (200 Lines). The amount on line 120 would be the amount owed at closing if there were no credits or if the deal were all cash. Most buyers have credits at closing and few pay the entire bill with a check.

Remember the deposit that accompanied the buyer's purchaser offer? Line 201 shows the deposit amount as a credit to the buyer.

The borrower's financing also shows up here. In the closing process, a mortgage is a credit because it reduces the amount owed by the purchaser.

If you agreed to pay $1,000 for roof repairs or promised to give the buyer a $3,000 credit for closing costs, this is where the money will appear.

In the 100 area we listed seller credits for items paid in advance. In the 200 area, we reverse the situation and list costs that the seller should have paid, but didn't. These items are a debit to the seller and a credit to the buyer.

Line 301 shows the gross amount due from the buyer and line 302 shows the purchaser's credits. The result is line 303, the amount the buyer must pay at closing.

While the buyer has heart failure looking at the bottom line, we can move over to the seller's side of the closing sheet and bask (we hope) in our good fortune.

Seller's Summary and Adjustments (400 Lines). This, for sellers, is where all the hard work pays off. Line 401 has the contract price, and to this amount adjustments for prepaid assessments and taxes are added. The result is line 420, the gross amount due to the seller.

Seller Reductions (500 Lines). While the gross amount due to sellers is a great and wonderful number, it is unlikely to be the final figure for the sale.

In the 500 lines there are deductions for settlement charges (line 1400 from the back of the form), mortgage payoffs to eliminate any current debt, and adjustments for unpaid taxes and assessments. In addition, if it is necessary to set up an escrow account for repairs, the amount will be shown in the 500 lines as a deduction from the seller's money.

In many areas, as well, money will be set aside for a water-bill escrow. The logic is that a final water bill may not be available at the time of closing and therefore money must be set aside to pay this cost. But why an escrow account for a water bill and not electricity or gas? The answer is that many water and sewage systems are owned by local communities and an unpaid bill is a lien against the property. Since a major purpose of closing is to make certain that unwanted liens have been removed, a water escrow account is established to pay off the final bill.

WHERE THE MONEY IS

If we take the gross amount owed to the seller, subtract assorted costs, the result is line 603, your cash from closing.

Now we know how much is owed to you from the sale of your home, but alas, we have a problem. In many settlements no check is issued at closing, a situation known as a "dry" settlement.

Where did the money go? Sometimes it's argued that the check cannot be disbursed until the title transfer has been recorded in the public records, perhaps in the next few days. In some cases it happens that the check is only available after, say, three o'clock on a Friday afternoon, a situation that means the check may not clear until Monday or Tuesday.

And, my gosh, who is getting the interest on that money while it languishes in an account? Not the buyer. Not the seller. Could it be the settlement provider? You bet.

The interest from the proceeds of settlement may not be a large sum of money by itself, but add together a few closings here and there, hold onto the money from each closing for a few extra days, and it becomes possible to have a huge bank balance that generates a hefty interest stream.

It's worth mentioning that in 1993 the Virginia Supreme Court ruled that the interest lawyers had been collecting from client escrow accounts should be paid to a foundation that provides legal aid and other benefits. Attorneys in the Commonwealth were not too thrilled and, in fact, one survey reportedly showed that 83 percent of those lawyers polled opposed the ruling, while a state banker's group argued that it was unconstitutional.

17
Taxes

While closing is the best moment of a successful real estate sale, the moment is fleeting. That big number at the bottom of the settlement sheet looks wonderful and you can bet that it will draw interest and admiration from a variety of sources, including some folks in government.

If you sell a home and have a profit, your gain is potentially taxable.

This single sentence leads us to a wonderful maze of definitions, deferrals, exceptions, and paperwork; enough complexity to cause eyestrain, headaches, and personnel shortages in the accounting field; and the realization that government is a partner in all we do.

Let us uncork the tax genie by stating that whatever you read in a book—including this one—is potentially wrong. The problem is that we have a dynamic tax system, one that can change overnight because of a court decision, tax code change, or new IRS policy. And to assure that matters are thoroughly confused, the tax implications of a sale are likely to differ depending on such factors as your individual income, write-offs, age, and where you move—among other factors.

Unfortunately, while the tax code may evolve instantaneously, books do not. They take time to write, edit, publish, distribute, and market. The entire process can span six months to a year, more than enough time for the tax system to be adjusted and revised in ways that may be important to you.

It thus becomes important before looking at tax issues to issue a critical piece of advice: use the information presented here to get a general idea of how the system works.

For specific advice and information, for advice and information that is up-to-date and appropriate for your particular situation, be certain to speak with a tax attorney, CPA, or enrolled agent. Do not rely on the content of this book, or any book, for specific tax advice.

Having waved a red flag that would be noticeable even in Moscow, let us now explore the wonderful world of home sales and taxes.

Is the check I got at closing my profit from the sale?
Probably not. To figure your profit, you have to ask if the house you sold was your first home or a later one.

If it was your first house, then you need to calculate how much it cost. In the eyes of the government, the cost of your home is determined by several factors.

1) Look at the original settlement sheet from when you bought the property. How much did you pay for the house? Are there settlement costs from when you bought the home that you have not otherwise written off? Add your undeducted closing costs to the sales price. $_____.

2) Have you made major improvements or repairs to your home such as a new addition? Did you save the receipts? If so, show the cost of long-term improvements. $_____.

3) What did you get from the sale? To figure your profit, take the sales price and subtract such selling expenses as brokerage fees, a point paid for the buyer, the expense of a deed release, etc. $_____.

4) Add items 1 and 2. $_____.

5) Subtract item 4 from item 3. This should be your profit on the sale of a first home. $_____.

Using the system above, here's how Mr. Gerkin figured his profit when he sold his home for $185,000.

> Item 1: Gerkin bought his home for $104,000 and had $3,600 in original closing expenses, a total of $107,600.
>
> Item 2: Gerkin added a new rec room at a cost of $6,000.
>
> Item 3: Gerkin sold his property for $185,000 but paid marketing expenses and settlement costs of $15,000, so his net result was $170,000.
>
> Item 4: If Gerkin adds item 1 ($107,600) and item 2 ($6,000), the total for item 4 is $113,600.
>
> Item 5: If Gerkin subtracts item 4 ($113,600) from item 3 ($170,000), the result is a taxable base of $56,400.

What if I owned a home before?
When you sold the last home, you filed a form 2119 with the IRS. This form showed your taxable profit from the last house you owned.

Add the old profit to the new profit from the latest sale.

Example: Gerkin had a $21,000 profit from the sale of an earlier home. The profit on the new sale is now $77,400 ($56,400 + $21,000).

If I have a profit, don't I owe a tax?

Maybe not. There are two basic issues to consider.

First, under the rollover residence replacement rule, if you buy a new prime residence of equal or greater value than the home you have just sold, and if you buy 24 months before the date of settlement or 24 months after the date of settlement, you must report your profit (form 2119), but *the tax is deferred—not eliminated.* (Active-duty military personnel have 48 months before the date of settlement and 48 months after the date of settlement to buy a home of equal or greater value and defer the tax.)

Second, if one or more of the owners is 55 years or older on the day of settlement, there is a one-time opportunity to write off as much as $125,000 in profits with the "over-55 rule." To qualify for this deduction the party 55 or older must have lived in the home as his or her principal residence during three of the past five years.

Suppose I sell my home this year, intend to buy another, but have yet to actually make a purchase. How do I report the profit?

It's a good idea to file IRS form 2119 with your taxes to document your situation. Complete the form and note that it is your intention to buy another home of equal or greater value within the allowable time period. If you do not buy a home of equal or greater value within the rollover rules, then you will have to pay a tax and possibly interest (because the tax was not paid in the year it was due).

My wife and I are both over 55. Can we each deduct $125,000?

No. One deduction per couple.

What if I'm divorced?

If during your marital years you or your spouse took the over-55 deduction then you cannot take it again.

We're both over 55 and we're not divorced, but we'd like to be. If we sell after the divorce can we each write off $125,000?

Yes.

We're an older couple and I've taken my over-55 deduction but my future spouse has not. If we marry will he lose his deduction?

Yes. If he now has property it may pay to have him sell and settle before the big day.

We're over 55 and when we sold our home we had a $90,000 profit. Can we write off the $90,000 now and later write off the remaining $35,000?

No. The over-55 rule can be used only once. If you write off $90,000, that's it.

We're over 55 and we expect to get married one day. We both have houses now. Can we both sell today and claim a $125,000 individual write-off? That's a total of $250,000.

You've got it. Until you marry you each may have the right to a one-time write-off.

I sold my home and before I could buy a new one of equal or greater value I was hit by a bus and wound up in a coma for five years. Do I have more time to buy a home and still qualify for the rollover tax break?

No.

I'm over 55. When I sell my home can I use both the replacement rule and the over-55 rule in the same year?

Yes.

I sold my house for $175,000. I had a $25,000 mortgage that was paid off at closing, leaving me with $150,000 in cash. Must I use that $150,000 to buy a home of equal or greater value?

No. You can stick the $150,000 in your pocket and finance the purchase of house #2 with a mortgage. The test is not where the cash goes, but whether home #2 is of equal or greater value when compared to home #1.

Our situation is different. We paid $50,000 for our home and sold it for $240,000 at a time when we were both over age 55. Our new home will cost $200,000. Do we owe taxes?

Given the figures in your question, you have a $190,000 profit. If $125,000 can be written off because of the over-55 rule, then $65,000 remains. The new property costs $200,000, which is more than $65,000, so taxes can be deferred. To figure the basis of your new home, subtract $65,000 from $200,000. The result is a taxable basis of $135,000—something you'll need to know when you sell the new home.

We are under 55. We sold our home for $185,000 and bought a new one for $165,000. Will we owe taxes?

Assuming the figures in your example are complete and final, you have bought a property that is neither equal nor higher in value than the first property. The $20,000 difference is likely to be taxable.

I refinanced my home four years ago and paid one point worth $2,000. My accountant says I can write off just $66.67 a year, so over four years I have deducted $266.68 ($66.67 × 4). How can I deduct the remaining $1,733.32 now that I have sold?

You can deduct the $1,733 in the year you sell or refinance the property.

When I buy my new house I will pay one point, or $2,500. Must that point be deducted over the term of the mortgage?

No. The government makes a distinction between points paid to acquire a home (which are deductible in the year paid) and points paid to refinance a personal residence (which are only deductible over the term of the mortgage).

Can I write off the mortgage interest and property taxes paid in the past year on the house I have sold?

Yes. Property taxes and allowable loan interest are deductible in the year paid.

Is there such a thing as loan interest that is not deductible?

Yes. As this is written, interest is only deductible in the usual case for loans of $1 million or less and home-equity loans valued at $100,000 or less. While such limits are not a problem for virtually all taxpayers, there are perpetual efforts in Washington to reduce or even eliminate mortgage interest write-offs.

I sold my home and have a loss. Now what?

While the government potentially taxes profits from the sale of a home, it does not generally allow you to deduct losses on the sale of a personal residence.

Isn't that unfair?

Next question.

Can I get a deduction for moving?

As a result of the 1993 tax bill, moving deductions are now severely limited.

To start, moving costs are only deductible if they are job-related; that is, you are moving to take new employment or because your job is being relocated. But, even job-related write-offs are banned unless the new employment site is at least 50 miles from the old one.

What about actual moving costs?

You can deduct whatever it costs to move personal effects and household goods.

Can I write-off such items as house-hunting expeditions, meals, and temporary living quarters?

Not any longer.

We sold at a loss because our home was hit by lightning. Do any special rules apply?

Yes. You may have a casualty loss, in which case write-offs are possible if they exceed insurance coverage. Speak to a tax adviser for details.

I use 10 percent of my home as an office and each year I have taken appropriate deductions. Will home office use affect my taxes?

The portion of your home used as a business does not qualify for the special tax benefits available to those who sell a prime residence. In essence, you have two properties for tax purposes. Ninety percent of your home is a principal residence and 10 percent is a business location subject to business tax regulations.

I am selling my home and taking back the financing. Do special rules apply?

You have an installment sale if you get at least one payment per year. The money paid to you will consist of "interest" that is taxable as regular income in the year received; "costs" that reflect the expense of buying the property, capital additions, and marketing expenses; and "profits" that may be protected by the rollover rule or the over-55 exemption. Be aware that special rules can apply if you sell to a relative.

Are there items on the closing sheet that are immediately deductible?

Probably. Costs on the closing sheet either reduce your sale profits or are deductible in the year paid. If you prepay property taxes, for example, that is a current deduction. It's best to take your settlement sheet to a tax adviser and to figure out what is now deductible, and what isn't.

Why pay taxes? I'm going to have a tax-free exchange and trade my home for a condo.

Good luck. The rules for tax-free exchanges do not apply when personal residences are involved.

What is a personal residence?

You would think that where you live is a personal residence. But what about someone who lives six months a year in Florida and six months in Montana? Which home is the personal residence?

For most people the definition of a prime residence is absolutely clear, but speak to a tax adviser if you live in more than one place for extended periods of time.

How long should I keep real estate records?

Unlike other tax records, which may have to be kept from three to six years, real estate files should be kept forever.

The reason is that you are likely to have a chain of sales and rollovers over many years that shelter real estate profits. You need the paperwork to show what was paid for a given property and how much you spent for capital improvements 20 years ago. There may also be estate issues where tax records are important.

In a related matter, please don't burn the mortgage if you pay it off. If the need arises, burn a copy.

Do state laws treat real estate sales differently than federal regulations?

Possibly. Check with a tax professional to assure that all state and local requirements have been met.

What if I don't report my home sale?

The party conducting settlement must report the transaction.

Where can I get more information?

Profits from a real estate sale can represent the equivalent of income earned over several years, so it pays to obtain proper advice from a knowledgeable professional. Tax attorneys, CPAs, and enrolled agents should all be regarded as qualified to handle tax matters. In addition, it pays to review various IRS forms and publications.

Form 2119: This is the form you must file when a home is sold.

Form 3903: This form is used to claim moving expenses.

Publication 521: Explains moving deductions and related matters.

Publication 523: Explores the wide world of tax considerations that arise when a home is sold.

Form 4868: The form needed to get an automatic extension so that returns can be filed late. Taxes, however, must be paid in a timely manner.

18
Additional Information

This book was written as a catalyst, a text designed to raise ideas, provide information, and suggest strategies that can have value for homesellers nationwide.

In addition, you may want to consider other ways to gain real estate information.

1) Speak to as many brokers and agents as possible. Many will have ideas and suggestions that have value.

2) Consider taking a basic, low-cost licensure class. Such classes—which can be available from colleges, universities, real estate organizations, and private schools—will show you how the real estate marketing system works in your jurisdiction and qualify you to take an agent's licensure test. The length of a licensure class will depend on the state where you live, but at this writing 45 to 120 clock hours of classroom training are common.

Once you finish a licensure class you can take a state test and become licensed, or you can simply use the information you receive to sell your home more effectively.

State rules typically require licensed brokers and agents to state in all literature and advertisements about the property that they, the owners, are licensed. :The purpose of this rule is to place other consumers on notice that they are dealing with a trained individual.

If you obtain an agent's license you may then be able to get a commission discount when you sell your home, and when you buy a new one, *depending on the arrangement you have with your broker*. If you sell a home for $200,000 *and* buy a home for $225,000 in a market where 6 percent commissions are common, then as much as $25,500 will go to brokers and their agents. If as a licensee you can cut commission expenses by a given percentage, then a significant number of dollars can be saved.

3) Read local newspapers. Many real estate sections offer solid advice and information, so clip and save the items most interesting to you.

4) Visit real estate expositions, particularly those sponsored by local newspapers, real estate organizations, and builder groups. Such expos often have a variety of booths, little or no selling pressure, plus a goodly amount of information.

5) Check out personal-finance publications such as *Money, Consumer's Digest,* and *Kiplinger Personal Finance* that often carry extensive, timely articles of value to homesellers.

6) If this guide has been helpful, then consider the other books in this series. *Successful Real Estate Negotiation* (with Douglas M. Bregman, Esq.), *Successful Real Estate Investing, Buy Your First Home Now,* and the latest annual edition of *The Common-Sense Mortgage (How to Cut the Cost of Home Ownership by $100,000 or More).* These books, published by HarperCollins, are available from booksellers nationwide.

7) Go electronic. Millions of people have a computer, modem, and mouse—all you need to be a part of the network nation. Local electronic bulletin boards may have real estate information, while a national service such as the real estate forum I host on America Online has an MLS open to brokers and non-brokers, current mortgage rates, real estate software for downloading, and online questions and answers. For additional information, call (800) 827-6364. *Be certain to mention extension 5764 for such free software, online time, and introductory pricing as may be available.*

8) Lastly, if you do well selling your home, pass on what you've learned and make the marketplace easier for the next person.

Glossary

Buried in every real estate deal are words and phrases that have special meaning to those who buy and sell property. The following glossary—originally developed for the HarperCollins guide *Successful Real Estate Negotiation*—describes words that homesellers will find of particular interest.

Acceptance:
A positive response to an offer or counter-offer. There are conditional acceptances ("I'll accept if you'll pay another $1,500 for the property"), express or written acceptances, implied acceptances ("I'm not going to say anything if you move in early"), and qualified acceptances ("I'll accept your offer subject to my lawyer looking at the deal").

Addenda:
Clauses, documents, or statements added to a contract that alter it in some way. To be enforceable, an addendum must be signed or initialed by both buyer and seller and clearly referenced in the body of the contract. For example, a contract might refer to an addendum by saying that "An addendum is attached to and made a part of this contract."

Addendum:
Singular of *addenda*

Agent:
Has two meanings in real estate. First, in general terms, someone who acts on behalf of another for a fee, such as a real estate broker or an attorney. Second, a type of real estate licensee who works under the authority of a real estate broker.

Appraisal:
An estimate of value produced by an appraiser. Appraisals are typically based on such factors as replacement costs, past sales of like properties, and the ability to produce income.

Appraiser:
A person familiar with local real estate values who estimates the worth of particular properties. Compensation for the appraiser cannot be related to a specific estimate of value ("I'll pay you $500 if you say the property is worth $150,000"), nor can the appraiser have an undisclosed interest in the property ("Come up with a good appraisal and you can act as a broker in the deal").

"As-Is" Agreements:
Situations where property is sold without warranty and in whatever physical condition it may be in as of the time a contract is signed. Before entering such deals, both buyers and sellers should check state and local regulations and warranty rules to see if and how "as-is" sales are affected by such laws.

Balloon Notes:
Real estate loans where some portion of the debt will remain to be paid off in a lump sum at the end of the loan term. Second trusts, for example, are frequently short-term loans (say three to five years), where a single large payment is due at the end of the loan term.

Brokers:
A licensed real estate professional employed by a buyer or seller to assist in a purchase or sale of real property. A broker's duties may include determining market values, advertising properties for sale, showing properties to prospective purchasers, assisting in the preparation of contracts, advising clients with regard to the acceptance or rejection of an offer or counter-offer, and dealing with a wide variety of related matters. While brokers have traditionally represented sellers, they can also be hired by purchasers, a concept known as "buyer brokerage." *For purposes of this guide, the term broker is often used in a general sense when either a broker or agent (or both) might be appropriate in certain situations.* For instance, a sentence saying that "brokers frequently spend many weeks working with prospects" could just as easily apply to agents.

Co-owners:
Two or more people with an interest in a single parcel of property. Co-ownership is an extremely important issue, since the form of co-ownership shown on a title may affect such matters as estates, inheritances, and personal liability in the event of a lawsuit.

Co-signer:
A person who signs and assumes joint liability with another. For instance, Mr. Daly may agree to co-sign a loan with his son so that a lender will provide a mortgage. Note that a co-signer may share liability to repay the loan but that such an individual is not necessarily a co-owner.

Contingent Contract:
A contract with a qualification or condition that must be resolved before the contract is final.

Contingency:
A provision that makes a contract conditional until a certain event occurs. For example, if buyer Lanham offers to purchase the Hartford property "subject to a structural inspection satisfactory to Purchaser," there is no enforceable contract unless Lanham says the structural inspection is satisfactory to him.

Contract:
In real estate, a binding, written agreement between two or more people to attain a common goal, typically the purchase or sale of property.

Credit Report:
A report from an independent source that outlines a person's creditworthiness by listing debts, liabilities, and related information. Used by lenders to assess the creditworthiness of potential borrowers. (Note: It's a good idea to check your own credit report on a regular basis to be sure that it's accurate. Contact local credit reporting agencies for more information.)

Damages:
An entitlement to compensation for a loss or injury. Damages may be recovered by any person who has suffered loss, detriment, or injury through an unlawful act, omission, or negligent act of another.

Deed:
A document that transfers title to real estate from one party to another and is recorded among the governmental land records in the jurisdiction where the property is located.

Deposit:
Usually money delivered by a buyer to a seller in advance of full performance to assure that the buyer's contract obligations will be fulfilled.

Easement:
A right to use someone else's property. Beware! Sometimes easements are created without an owner's permission or knowledge.

Encroachment:
An intrusion, obstruction, or invasion of someone else's property. For example, if a neighbor just built a fence and the fence is six inches over your property line, it's an encroachment.

Fixtures:
Items that usually convey to the buyer in a realty transaction unless specifically excluded from the sale. Fixtures are generally attached to the property and intended to be a part of the property. Examples of common fixtures include built-in dishwashers, furnaces, chandeliers, and plumbing.

Gift:
The voluntary transfer of money, property, or something of value from one person to another without any duty or expectation of repayment. Since gifts in the context of a real estate transaction may be large, donors should check with a CPA or tax attorney before making a gift commitment to assure that all tax consequences are understood.

Inspection:
An examination to determine the condition or quality of any aspect of a real estate transaction.

Language of Art (Legal Wording):
Standardized language with specific legal meanings. A trap for the unwary, legal language may contain definitions, meanings, shadings, and implications not found when the same words are used in everyday conversation.

Loan Origination Fee:
A fee charged by lenders to cover loan processing costs, often equal to 1 percent of the loan's value.

Merge:
To absorb or fuse one document or right into another. In real estate, this usually means the sales contract is merged into or becomes a part of the deed. Once this merger takes place, the terms of the real estate contract are no longer in effect. However, if a real estate contract says that a portion of the document—or the complete document—is to "survive," then that material will not be merged into the deed.

Offer:
A proposal that, when accepted, will become a contract. In real estate the buyer commonly makes a written offer to purchase property, which may then be accepted, rejected, or countered by the seller. Offers may be withdrawn without penalty at any time prior to acceptance, unless the offer provides otherwise. If a proposal is rejected, it may not be resurrected without permission of the person who made the offer.

Option:
A right to act under certain terms and conditions. For example, if Mr. Clermont can purchase the Mullin property for $150,000 if he acts by June 1, he has an option. If he does not act by June 1, the option is expired.

Points (Loan Discount Fees):
An interest fee charged by lenders at settlement equal to 1 percent of a mortgage. The purpose of points is to raise the lender's yield above the apparent interest rate.

Quitclaim Deed:
A deed that says, in effect, "whatever title I have, I hereby give to you." Unfortunately, the seller who offers a quitclaim deed may have no rights or interests to sell. *Always consult an attorney before agreeing to any deal that involves a quitclaim deed.*

Remedies:
Forms of compensation, such as money or actions, that are granted by a court in response to a wrongful situation or condition.

Satisfaction:
Acceptance by one or both parties on the completion of an obligation. As an example, Mr. Brody offers to buy the Kent residence if he decides the roof inspection is satisfactory. If he accepts the inspection report, the contract will be finalized.

Settlement (Closing):
The act or process of adjusting and finalizing all dealings, money, and arrangements for real estate buyers and sellers. At settlement, all adjustments are made as of the date of the settlement, all money is properly disbursed, the deed is prepared with the new owner's name, and the property is conveyed in accordance with the terms of the contract and the intentions of the parties.

Subject To:
An offer or contract that depends on a separate condition or action. In real estate, this phrase is usually found in a provision such as "This property is being sold subject to a right-of-way granted to the electric company allowing its electrical lines to cross the front yard."

Survey:
An examination of the boundaries of real property and the improvements on it. A survey can reveal the quantity of land, boundary distances, the location of improvements on the property such as the house, and other vital information about the property.

Tenancies:
Interests in real estate defined in the deed. A vitally important matter that shows how title to the property is held.

Tenant:
An individual or entity, such as a business, that occupies someone else's property. Note that while "tenancies" usually describe forms of property ownership, a "tenant" does not own property.

Termites:
Wood-boring insects that can infest and damage homes. Most realty sales require a termite inspection showing the property is free and clear of termites and other wood-boring insects. Such inspections should also list insect damage, if any.

Title:

The right of property ownership. Such ownership can be held solely, jointly, or in common. In many states title can be held in corporate or in partnership form.

Title Insurance:

Policies purchased at settlement, which ensure that one's ownership or interest in the property is protected against loss if a title defect is found or if title claims are made after ownership is transferred. Policies differ and may contain exclusions and exceptions. Also, policy coverage may be expanded to include additional protection. Speak to the person conducting settlement for complete information.

Warranties:

Guarantees, promises, and protections provided by one party to another. In real estate contracts, there are usually warranties regarding the condition of the appliances and certain fixtures. New homes often have extensive warranties covering not only fixtures and appliances but the overall structure of the house as well. There can be "express" (written) warranties, "implied" warranties (guarantees that the parties intended even though they may not have stated them specifically in the contract), and "imposed" warranties (guarantees created, for example, by state law).

Index

About the Author

Peter G. Miller, a nationally recognized real estate authority, has experience as a real estate broker, investor, and journalist. He is a columnist with *The Real Estate Professional*, host of the real estate area with America Online, and author of such leading books as *The Common-Sense Mortgage, Buy Your First House Now, Successful Real Estate Investing,* and *Successful Real Estate Negotiation* (with Douglas M. Bregman).